The *Abba* FORMATION

Dr. Kerry Wood
with Dr. Chiqui Wood

Cover Design: Ivethe Zambrano-Fernández
wwwdesignbytwo.com

Photography of Author by John Choate

Bedford, Texas
www.BurkhartBooks.com

Dedication

To Pastor Jack Hayford

Pastor Jack, as he is most affectionately known, has received many honors for the impact he has made on the Body of Christ at large, Christian-Jewish relations, racial and denominational relations, and bridge-building attempts between factions in the Evangelical Church. He is known as a torchbearer to mobilize Christian Men in stadiums across America, and for his local impact upon the faith and business community in his own greater Los Angeles area.

For almost forty years I have known Pastor Jack as a voice of soundness in blending faith and reason, passion and sobriety, and the balance of the Spirit and the Word. In the earliest season of my ministry—youth ministry to be exact—I had been strongly influenced by one of the streams of the Charismatic Renewal known by some as "The Word Movement." There was strong emphasis on teaching the Word of God with a confirming witness of God's power. After a few years, however, I began to ask the Lord for a broader expression of His Word. I was seeking a way to declare the truth of the Spirit and the Word in ways that investigated all of Scripture, book by book, and cover to cover.

I first saw Jack Hayford on Christian television, and as I suppose was the case with many, his reasoned pastoral approach coupled with His passion for Spirit-fullness immediately left me wanting to hear more. I became a member of The Church On The Way tape of the month club and eventually had boxes full of cassette tapes and series. It became my daily bread to such a degree that I have considered Pastor Jack my own pastor for several decades now.

I eventually attended one of Pastor Jack's Autumn Leadership Conferences. This was my first visit to the famed church. That conference led me to attend the School of Pastoral Nurture, which led to The King's University Master of Divinity program, which led to the Doctor of Ministry at The King's (just before the main campus was moved to Southlake, Texas, and Gateway Church).

Why the personal history? Because no man—with the exception of my own father—has impacted my life more than Pastor Jack. He opened his home to those of us that studied under him. He opened his heart to freely give away everything he had received. Tens of thousands of pastors have been touched by him, just as I have, yet he never pointed to himself, but always to Jesus. Integrity of heart and a passion for fullness have always been his life and message. Though I take full responsibility for my own words, thoughts, and theology in my writings, and will never be as clear or articulate as Pastor Jack, I hope you, dear reader, will understand that I learned from him, but never enough. He has never sought praise or approval, but I am eternally grateful that the Lord answered my prayers for someone who could take me deeper. Thank you, Pastor Jack, for your humility, passion, integrity, and the living witness of starting well and finishing well. You've given us all hope.

Acknowledgments

My wife, Chiqui, cares deeply about the stewardship of the truths the Lord has invested into me. Because of that care (and our love for sharpening each other) she challenges me on how ideas are articulated. This is a great gift to me, and certainly to you the reader. Words cannot express my appreciation for such a joy-filled partner in life. In addition, many thanks to Patsy Moore, Phil Strickland, and Donna Burley for their feedback and editing skills, and for a partner like Tim Taylor at Burkhart Books who serves so many, so well.

If you have not done so already, you will want to obtain the companions to this last volume of three in a trilogy by Chiqui and me. The first is *The Abba Foundation* (Dr. Chiqui Wood's theological foundations to everything I offer in the other two volumes). Her volume is critical because we will apply sonship ideas in wrong ways if we don't have an accurate view of the nature of the Father. Sonship, after all, is all about how we relate to the Father. The second is *The Abba Factor*, in which we contrast the orphan spirit to the spirit of sonship and make numerous applications. This third volume moves from the causes and external results to the Holy Spirit's role in the internal process of our transformation. This series also makes for a great home group or Bible study series. *The Abba Journey* workbook is available with extra questions and supplemental background material.

Finally, many thanks to Tod and Tammy Williams for their generosity in sharing their luxurious Twelve Stones cabin (Broken Bow, OK) as our writing haven. Their gift of hospitality has refreshed our souls.

Contents

Preface

When God gives himself, either flesh is inspired, or Spirit is enfleshed. In the Old Testament, man's spirit was inhabited by the nature of death and could not host the glory of God. God's Spirit would come upon the prophets and inspire them to speak or to work, but did not abide. But God's kind of love requires a paracleting withness that can only be realized by incarnation. In the New Testament, after the resurrection of Christ, Jesus breathed on His disciples in the Capernaum upper-room and said, "Receive the Spirit" (John 20:22), and they were born again. This is the replay, the do-over of "the first breath" when God formed Adam of the dust of the ground and breathed into him the breath of life (Gen. 2:7). These disciples (and all those who would come thereafter) are not just inspired but indwelt by the Spirit of God.

You and I do not live for an occasional inspirational moment, but an ongoing indwelling—an incarnation, an enfleshment—of the Spirit.

Our God is not happily distant, content in some unreachable otherness. Father, Son and Spirit are patiently but tenaciously determined to infuse all of creation with Spirit, until the rocks, trees, and stars are no longer groaning but alive with glorious eternal harmonies of fulfilled purpose (both J.R.R. Tolkien and C. S. Lewis were onto something with their visions of animated nature). Yet, God willingly waits for His creation to be brought to life by the manifestation of those sons He had originally established as joint rulers over "all the works of His hands" (Ps. 8:3-8). God apparently loves the Imago Dei free will as much as incarnation.

This is the tension of time and history and our internal groanings (Rom. 8:22-23). God is not hassled by time—He stands outside of it, but lovingly works within it. The result was the resurrection, and with it the realization of eternal union between body and spirit, human and divine. Creation is yet waiting, groaning, for the sons and daughters of God to rise to their place again. The Holy Spirit is tenaciously, patiently, almost imperceptibly working to restore you and me to that place. Within these pages, I believe, are the means whereby we can accelerate that process of transformation—speed the work of the Spirit by cooperation– so as not to settle for occasional inspirational moments, but a new order of the enfleshment, the realized indwelling of the Spirit in sonship.

The sons of God are walking the earth again, the groans destined to become praise.

Kerry Wood

Introduction

This life in Christ is an inside-out life. It starts in the deepest part of you and overflows to the rest of you because the same Spirit who raised Christ from the dead lives in us and is the generating power of our lives. We are not pastoring our old nature. We are not counseling a corpse. We are living out of a new place, and that place is a Person. We are not working primarily at the psychological level, but deeper yet, in the very heart, the spirit of man. We learn to wash our minds with the living waters that overflow from our spirits, not by willpower but by the infinite, overflowing power of the Spirit of God. This is *The Abba Formation*.

I hope that you have read *The Abba Factor* and *The Abba Foundation* and are ready to go deeper to the actual process of transformation. This volume is built upon the foundation of the previous two, and I suggest you read *The Abba Factor* before proceeding, if possible. *The Abba Formation* goes almost immediately to the internal world of our spirits and begins to delve into the work of the indwelling Holy Spirit, who is lovingly but tenaciously gardening the soil of our souls, uprooting the tares the enemy has sown there (to use Jesus' imagery), and building and planting those things the Father has prepared for us.

We will take you to a place in the Scriptures that is too seldom discussed —1 Corinthians 2—where Paul articulates a clear contrast between what could be known under the Old Covenant and what is now revealed under the New Covenant by the giving of the Spirit. We'll examine two kinds of knowledge: one that is life-giving and one that is deceptive and empty.

In Chapter Three we will consider what Jesus had in mind when calling us to return to childlikeness, and how that work of the Spirit is nothing less than being restored to a form of genius we didn't even realize we had lost. We will consider the latest scientific research that shows very real damage is done to the brain, body, and even DNA of children who suffer adverse childhood experiences, and the long-term health impacts as those children become adults. The damage is so deep and pervasive, this question must be answered, "Can transformation actually occur when the impacts are that severe?" Though I am neither a scientist nor a psychologist, I will suggest that the scientific verification of these natural impacts to childhood will help us understand spiritual realities.

In Chapter Four we see that it is not willpower, but the Gardener of the Soul, who is uprooting the old ways of thinking. Chapters Five through Seven examine the practical connection with our spirits and our words as the God-designed means of both filling and releasing life. The final chapters address how this new life works its way to our intended purpose—the partnering with the Father's mission to see many sons come back to the Father.

The central reality of sonship, of course, is that redemption is about nothing less than a whole new creation, and no small part of that redemption is a process. Therefore, the objective of this book is to unfold practical ways to cultivate ongoing transformation that makes every fear, failure, and foothold of the past the target of the Holy Spirit's precise operations. Before we get into the transformation process, note the clear contrast of what the outcome will look like.

Review: Contrasting Sons to Orphans

	Son's Thinking	Orphan's Thinking
Image of God	Sees God as loving Father	Sees God as master
Relational	Interdependent, acknowledges need	Independent and self-reliant
Spiritual Orientation	Law of love	Love of the law
Emotional Orientation	Rest and peace	Insecure, lack of peace, busy cover
Need for Approval	Knows he is accepted in God's love	Strives for praise, approval, and acceptance of man
Motivation for Service	Deep gratitude for the unconditional love of God	Seeks personal achievement to impress others and earn his place
Motivation of Christian Disciplines	Pleasure and delight to be with Father	Duty, payment, or no motivation at all
Motivation for Purity	Protect the Father-son relationship	Tool to earn God's blessing
Self-Image	Positive and affirmed, value set by God	Root of rejection or pride from comparing self to others

Source of Comfort	Father's embrace in quietness and worship	Seeks comfort in counterfeit affections: possessions, position, passion or power
Peer Relationships	Humility; able to value others as sons, rejoicing in their blessing and success	Competition: rivalry, jealousy, critical of others' success or blessing
Other's Faults or Performance	Empathy: love covers as sons seek to restore in meekness	Exposure: in order to make oneself look better in comparison, faultfinding
View of Authority	Respectful: honoring them as extensions of Father's love	Distrustful: source of pain, lack of heart submission
Correction	Receiving as a means of maturing toward partnership in Father's business	Easily offended: performance orientation puts priority on being right
Expressions of Love	Open, affectionate, nurturing	Guarded and conditional
Mindset	Liberty and boldness	Bondage and brashness/timidity
Focus/Vision	To enjoy Father's love and represent Father's love to others	Ambition: strives for recognition and achievement to be counted among sons
Goals	To enjoy the Father as inheritance	To gather and consume inheritance

In *The Abba Factor* we examined an in-depth process that leads to an orphan spirit and the transformational process that The Holy Spirit works in us to bring us to an awareness of our sonship. Ultimately, what is true in our spirits by the new birth (a way a being), must become a way of believing and behaving. It is not enough to obtain some good teachings on sonship and the orphan spirit. It is not enough to get familiar with the language and make the assumption that hearing a concept with the

Freedom is not a place to get to but a way of being and belonging that is already yours. mind is equal to being transformed in spirit. Teaching alone, even reading this book, cannot change the internal "want-tos" so the past will no longer hound our thoughts, memories or appetites. It requires a daily partnership with the Holy Spirit. Perhaps you did not grow up hearing much about the Holy Spirit. You are not alone. He has been so ignored that He has been called "the Forgotten God."[1] However, Jesus talked plainly about Him and told all His followers that a relationship with The Holy Spirit would be essential for us to fulfill our mission and ministry (John 16:7-11).

The Abba Formation takes you to a daily relationship equipped with daily practices (encounter triggers) that keep you full, overflowing, and fruitful. My prayer for you is that, by the Spirit, you embrace an understanding that freedom is not a place to get to but a way of being and belonging that is already yours. Though it may not look like it yet:

Now are we the sons of God.

1 John 3:3

Paul says:

For we know that the whole creation has been groaning together in the pains of childbirth until now. And not only the creation, but we ourselves, who have the first-fruits of the Spirit, groan inwardly as we wait eagerly for adoption as sons.

Romans 8:22-23

I like the way J. B. Phillips finishes this thought: *"…which will mean that at last we have realized our full sonship in Him."*

As a final introductory note, Masculine terms and pronouns (e.g. sonship) are not intended to exclude women. These truths apply to women just as much as men. The use of masculine terms throughout is just to simplify grammatical issues (not having to say he/she, his/her at every turn) so we can focus more easily on what the Spirit is saying.

Finally, know that I will repeat myself at various points along the way. Please excuse the teacher in me that seeks to embed the ideas deeply. Come along now– let's open the priceless gifts we've already been given.

One

Deep Calls to Deep

Deep calls unto deep at the noise of Your waterfalls; All Your waves and billows have gone over me.

– Psalms 42:7

What is the *Abba Cry*? *Abba* (Daddy), along with *Imma* (Mommy), are Aramaic words also used in Jewish culture. These are the first words an Aramaic-speaking child would learn and, as such, represent the language of infancy. Gordon Fee asserts that the *Abba Cry* is a lifelong cry to God as our Heavenly Father. He says it was "the endearing term that children of all ages continued to use, expressing both intimacy and special relatedness. What may begin as baby talk is not thereby to be outgrown, on the contrary, to be grown into."[2] That we are the beloved children of the eternal God is a knowledge that is shed abroad in our hearts by the Spirit (Rom. 5:5) and by that same Spirit is manifest in our lifelong cry to God as our heavenly *Abba*.[3]

The *Abba Cry* Replaces the Lie

Let's begin with an important story of inheritance lost and inheritance restored. Do you remember the story of Mephibosheth? Perhaps not. He was an unknown, nondescript person. He could have been somebody but was a nobody. He was a could've-been, should've-been, would've-been … if only his daddy hadn't died a premature death. His daddy was Jonathan, the son of King Saul. Mephibosheth could have been king one day. He had royalty in his blood but when we read his story in 2 Samuel 9, we find him living in squalor.[4]

Mephibosheth is the prototypical picture of the orphan spirit. He had no father image in his childhood and the scriptural account gives no intimation that he grew up with a mother. His life was interpreted to him by malevolent informants who didn't know or trust David. His early traumatic experiences only seemed to validate what he had been told about his victimization. He grew up in a wasteland far different than his blood-lineage promised. He learned mistrust of authority and how to manipulate relationships. In a city of refuge, where the city motto is "no honor among thieves," he learned to look out for number one. Fear ruled his life, but he probably gave the appearance of being "in control." The "progression of the orphan spirit" is practically tattooed on Mephibosheth (see *The Abba Factor*, Chapters 5 and 6).

If you have been around church much, you know the story of David rising to power with the favor of God upon him, and in time entering a heart-to-heart covenant with Jonathan, the son of King Saul. The Bible says David and Jonathan loved each other so much that they were as one soul, so they entered into covenant with one another. That Hebrew covenant testified that both partners considered the other's family to be as his own. It said, in essence, "If I'm ever in a fight you'll fight for me, and if you're ever in a fight I'll fight for you." That covenant of brotherly love meant, "All that is yours is mine, and all that is mine is yours." Jonathan and David were covenant brothers.

Jonathan and Saul, however, died prematurely. As a result of Saul's insecurities, the palace had been inundated with lies about David and what he would do to the royal family if he ever caught them.[5] This is just the way life was back then. When a new king who was not in the order of the royal bloodline took the throne, he would customarily slaughter all remaining family members of the previous king to rid himself of opposition. As the palace servants fled at the news of Saul's death and David's imminent approach, the nurse dropped Jonathan's son, Mephibosheth. The lad grew up a cripple as a result of these injuries. His life unfolded in hiding in a little city of refuge called Lodebar.[6]

Lodebar means "a wasteland, no pasture, a desert place."[7] In the cities of refuge there was little trust of authority. It was every man for himself—a den of robbers and thieves who were looking out for each other and mostly for themselves. The common language among fugitives is lies. They've believed and told lies about their parents, the government, their king, and themselves. One can tell a lie so much that he believes it himself. This city of refuge was a waste place—no pasture, wasted dreams and wasted lives. You can imagine what Mephibosheth had grown up hearing about King David. In 2 Samuel 9 we find him living in this state, unaware that his fate was about to change forever.

Not long into his reign, David awakens one morning with an ache in his soul for his deceased blood-brother, Jonathan. He says to his servants, "Is there anyone left in Saul's house that I can show kindness to for the sake of my brother Jonathan?" (2 Sam. 9:1). Ziba, one of Saul's former servants, is summoned and relates that Mephibosheth is still alive and in a city of refuge called Lodebar, in the desert.

Here's the irony: Mephibosheth was in covenant with the King of Israel but didn't know it.

What Mephibosheth had hoped would never happen, does. There comes a knock on Mephibosheth's door. Someone looks through the peep hole and says, "It's the servant of the King!" Mephibosheth's heart pounds with fear, certain that his head is about to roll. He had heard all his life what a blood-thirsty man King David is. Do you suppose anyone even knew or bothered to tell him that David and Jonathan were in covenant or that David had committed himself to Jonathan's household and future? Here's the irony: Mephibosheth was in covenant with the King of Israel but didn't know it. He had believed a lie and had plenty of voices around him to interpret authority in his life as personal rejection.

The obedient servant, Ziba, however, brings Mephibosheth to the King. Mephibosheth is taken by royal carriage back to the King's palace, and with crutches under his arms and fear in his eyes, he hobbles into the great hall. As soon as he sees David he falls on the floor, and says, "I'm just a dead dog. I'm worthless. Whatever you're going to do to me, do it quickly."

Please notice that when the pressure is really on, what people really believe about themselves comes out. But in the midst of Mephibosheth's transparent confession of the lies he has believed, the real truth—the unthinkable, unimaginable good news—breaks in upon the unsuspecting orphan.

Can you imagine what a shock and wonder it must have been for Mephibosheth when David, with a loving smile on his face picks him up, sits him on a chair and says, "This place is your place. You will eat at my table for the rest of your life; not only that, but I've saved all the land that belonged to your father and your father's father, for you. All of it is yours, and you'll never have to work one day to earn it. My servants will take care of you and you will eat until you are full. You are now my son." Mephibosheth's orphan head was spinning.

All Are Crippled

The truth is, we all as Adam's race came crippled into the world—separated from God and susceptible to the lies that are told about Him. All have sinned and come short of His glory (Rom. 3:23). A deceiver has blinded the minds of men that we would not see the glorious light of the Good News. The deceiver has lied about God until the whole planet is under the darkness of deception. "If God exists at all," this father of lies says, "He is out to punish you for your sins." No matter how good of a home life you were raised in, there is a Lodebar-wasteland mentality perpetrated by "the god of this world."

> *But even if our gospel is veiled, it is veiled to those who are perishing,*
> *whose minds the god of this age has blinded, who do not believe,*
> *lest the light of the gospel of the glory of Christ,*
> *who is the image of God, should shine on them.*
>
> 2 Corinthians 4:3-4

In the same way David entered covenant with Jonathan, Jesus took on humanity and became the embodiment of union between God and man. Being fully God and fully man, Jesus' body would provide the blood of the covenant that makes a way for orphans to come home. Dear friend, never underestimate the power and preciousness of the incarnation. For it was in Jesus, the Son of God coming to this world and becoming the son of man, that God forever committed Himself to the human dilemma. What's more, the incarnation, God's forever-covenant to be with humanity and for humanity, cannot be reversed.

The Holy Spirit knocks on our door and gently brings orphan-minded sons and daughters back to the King's palace. The Holy Spirit is the One who convinces and convicts us of a reality we dared not believe or imagine—that we were born for royalty. And it's the Holy Spirit (pictured as Ziba in this story) that will take care of us, slowly transforming our orphan thinking into the mindset of son-kings. It is the Holy Spirit who has already begun disbursing the gifts of our inheritance, which is only the down-payment of what unfolds for sons and daughters of God for the rest of eternity.

The incarnation, God's forever-covenant to be with humanity and for humanity, cannot be reversed.

You and I have found out what it's like to share this message. We have a wonderful Father, who by His overflowing love has created a beautiful and bountiful world (and cosmos) for His children. We all resonate with the part of Mephibosheth's story that something was wrong early on. In some way we have felt crippled by life, but will we believe the rest of the story? Can you hear the knock on your door? Do you dare peek through the peep hole and see that The Holy Spirit has come to take you to the palace? Some would say, "I believe that story is true. I believe that is me. I've been crippled by life, and yet I have something inside of me that says I'm linked up with the King of the earth. I'm living in a wasteland, but I know I belong in a palace." There are also some who say skeptically, "Who are you trying to fool? You're just bound up in those religious ideas; you just need a crutch. Don't you know that if you're going to make it in this world you have to get tough and make it on your own?"

How Do I Replace the Lie?

The reality is, you can't replace the lie. The futility of humanistic psychology (though not all psychology is practiced from a humanistic perspective), is the notion that somehow, I can force myself, by sheer will and good training, to think different thoughts. "Just use your willpower and resolve to not think that way anymore," the humanist mantra beats on. You can hear it from the pulpits of the land as well, "Change your thoughts, and you change your habits. What you can conceive you can achieve," they say. It sounds good. It sounds powerful and resonates because we were made to be powerful. The truth is, if you had the power to replace the lie, you would have done so already, but willpower runs out because man was never designed to run on willpower. We are, first, spirit beings, not volitional/emotional beings at the core. You are a spirit. You were designed to run on spiritual power, not willpower. If humanity could eradicate its own evil desires, our societies would be getting brighter and brighter.

What psychology brings to the table is that changing the way we think about ourselves is a process. It's rarely ever a zap coming from heaven, and suddenly I see all things clearly and have a renewed mind about my redeemed reality. Mephibosheth sat down at King David's table that day, but do you think he instantly walked away from all the lies he had grown up with or had instant and total trust of David? No. However, what psychology tries to

The deepest place of man is not in the brain, since the brain is physical matter, but a non-material reality called spirit. reshape at the "head" level, the Holy Spirit comes to transform where transformation really happens—at the heart level, in the "knower."

This is why New Year's resolutions don't last, and everyone knows it. Diets don't lead to permanent change, and everyone knows it. A positive mental attitude can't be sustained under pressure, and everyone knows it. They just don't know why. I submit to you that when our culture embraces the fundamental lie that we are psychological beings and the result of a godless evolution, we forsake the basic understanding that we are eternal spirit beings made in the image of God. When we believe that the deepest seat of man is in the brain, then ultimately materiality (not the spirit) is at our core.

God is a spirit (John 4:24) and we worship Him in spirit and truth, because we are spirit. Before the material universe was created, God is. God breathed spirit into man, creating eternal fellowship. Therefore, the deepest place of man is not in the brain, since the brain is physical matter, but a non-material reality called "spirit." The New Testament calls it "the hidden man of the heart" (1 Pet. 3:4), "the inward man" (2 Cor. 4:16), and the spirit (1 Thess. 5:23). That is where the Spirit of God comes to reside, and man is born again. Jesus said man is born of flesh (a natural birth) and of Spirit (a spiritual birth) (John 3:6). This is where real transformation happens. So, it is the Holy Spirit that displaces the lies that we have believed by an empowered experience in the Truth, thereby creating within us both the desires and the power to do what is pleasing to the Father (Phil. 2:13).

It is the Holy Spirit that displaces the lies that we have believed by an empowered experience in the Truth, thereby creating within us both the desires and the power to do what is pleasing to the Father (Phil. 2:13).

Willpower Is Insufficient

Paul's primary contrast to help believers see what it means to be "in Christ" is to show the powerlessness of the human will to master the spiritual powers of sin. Sin is not mastered by willpower. Thus, the point of Romans 7—"The thing I want to do, I can't do, and the very thing I don't want to do is exactly what I end up doing ..."—is to show that trying to keep the Law by willpower is futile. Without the Spirit, no one can keep the Law. His rhetorical question at the end of that chapter, *"Oh wretched man that I am! Who shall deliver me from this body of death?"* is answered by:

> *The Law of the Spirit of Life in Christ Jesus has made me free from the Law of sin and death.*
>
> Romans 8:2

In other words, your willpower and sincere intentions will run out before Satan's temptations do. So, give the battle over to the Eternal Spirit, the Holy Spirit, the indwelling Spirit, who never gets weary and provides you with a spirit of faith so that you mortify (put to death) the deeds and appetites of the flesh by the Spirit (not by willpower).

The Apostle John tells us that it is the Holy Spirit that teaches us at a deeper place in our being than our conscious thoughts. He says:

> *But you have an anointing from the Holy One, and you know all things ... But the anointing which you have received from Him abides in you, and you do not need that anyone teach you.*
>
> 1 John 2:20, 27

Moreover, Jesus himself says:

> *It is written in the prophets, "And they shall all be taught by God."*
>
> John 6:45

Imagine you were a student in one of my university classes and I sent in a substitute to teach all the lectures and even give the Final Exam study questions. The problem is, the substitute teacher only speaks in a language you don't understand. In fact, the substitute speaks a language no one in the class understands! You would want your money back, right? How would you learn? How would you know what is on the Final? This is where humanity is. The spirit realm is the spirit of reality, but we've been trying to learn who we are and what we do in the language of the natural world. We have settled for a shadow of the real and get frustrated that we can't find fulfillment. The answers to humanity's problems are "in the Spirit." As tenacious as we are to build our towers to Babel to prove we can solve the problems and keep man moving toward this imagined social evolution, the larger the problems become and each generation more despairing than the last. But there is a way to know.

Two Kinds of Knowing, Two Locations

If we take the Scriptures seriously, then we must understand that there are two kinds of knowing that we experience. There is a knowing at the mental (*psuche*) level, which is conscious and cognitive, and a knowing at the spirit (*pneuma*) level which is sub-conscious, even preconceptual. Likewise, there are two kinds of information—natural information that comes to us through our five physical senses, and spiritual information that comes to our spirits, and through our spirits, by the Holy Spirit. Jesus said:

The words that I speak to you are spirit [pneuma],
and they are life [zōē].

John 6:63

God reveals this two-fold reality to us very early on in the Scriptures by introducing the concept of the Tree of Life and the Tree of the Knowledge of Good and Evil. One gives life; the other kills. Paul says similarly:

The letter kills, but the Spirit gives life.

2 Corinthians 3:6

As concise as the Scriptures are on this, and as clear as Jesus was that the Holy Spirit would come into our spirits to teach us (John 16:12-15), we continue, both inside and outside the Church, to seek spiritual life and personal transformation through head knowledge and information gleaned through the senses.

How many conferences and seminars do we have to attend before we realize that the key to "success" is not centered in best practices, methods, and metrics, but in obedience to a living word from God, breathed in our hearts by the Holy Spirit, that creates something that is life-giving and eternal in the hearer?

I want to tell you plainly—information in your head (mind) has no power to transform you. *It is revelation in your spirit by the Holy Spirit that transforms you from the inside out.* Don't let that scare you. The wonderful news is that this is not something you can do, but the Holy Spirit who formed you in your mother's womb knows exactly how to do this in you. You only need to learn to listen.

Information in your head (mind) has no power to transform you. It is revelation in your spirit by the Holy Spirit that transforms you from the inside out.

By now you may be saying, "OK, I get it. This *Abba* thing is really about the Holy Spirit, so just tell me what to do. Give me the answer already! What are the three easy steps to make this happen?" Those are still the wrong questions. First, we are still asking for information to appease our inquiring mind. Secondly, it's not a what or a how, but a Who. Let's look at how the Holy Spirit teaches us by revelation and replaces the lies we have believed with the truth to convince us of our sonship. (I hope you will stay with me, but if you just have to skip to the "to do" chapter, look at Chapter 5, the Language of Sonship, and then come on back to the Who. If you get the *Who*, He'll get you to the *what* and *how*.)

A Change in Strategy

We get the clearest picture of how this works from the Apostle Paul who understood the death-dealing power of the Law all too well. In writing to the Corinthian believers, he is reflecting upon his first occasion with them. He had come from Mars Hill in Athens, where he used the rhetorical skills in wisdom (*sophia*) to reach out to the philosophy-lovers in Athens. He preached to them about "the unknown god" (Acts17). It was an ingenious strategy, as human strategy goes, but he saw little spiritual fruit from it. Some called him a babbler, some mocked, and a few joined him (Acts 17:34). Paul left Athens and went to Corinth.

Something happened in Paul's heart on the way to Corinth, because when he arrived he changed his strategy. Instead of using the eloquent speech of Mars Hill, he took a different approach. He explains:

> *For I determined not to know anything among you except Jesus Christ and Him crucified ... And my speech and my preaching were not with persuasive words of human wisdom* [sophia], *but in demonstration of the Spirit and of power.*
>
> 1 Corinthians 2:2, 4

The Gospel of Jesus is not fully proclaimed until it has been demonstrated, for it is a Gospel of power by the Holy Spirit.

Yes, we could say that Paul knew his audiences and determined a different strategy for Corinth because it was a different audience, but that doesn't explain why he would say as he does in verse 5:

> *… that your faith should not be in the wisdom of men, but in the power of God.*
> 1 Corinthians 2:5

Paul saw that preaching the Gospel is more than telling a culturally relevant story about Jesus. He understood that the Gospel of Jesus is not fully proclaimed until it has been demonstrated, for it is a Gospel of power by the Holy Spirit.

Please don't miss the connection with the demonstration of the Spirit's power and the necessary affective experience that comes with such a demonstration. The enemy uses experiences to lie to you about your identity. By contrast, the Holy Spirit will use divinely-empowered experiences to replace those lies with the Truth.

What Paul says next is so crucial to our understanding of how the Holy Spirit processes the awareness of our sonship, that I am asking you to read it through right now as if it is the first time you have ever seen it.

> *And my speech and my preaching were not with persuasive words of human wisdom [sophia], but in demonstration of the Spirit and of power, that your faith should not be in the wisdom of men, but in the power of God.*

> *However, we speak wisdom among those who are mature, yet not the wisdom of this age, nor of the rulers of this age, who are coming to nothing. But we speak the wisdom of God in a mystery, the hidden wisdom which God ordained before the ages for our glory, which none of the rulers of this age knew; for had they known, they would not have crucified the Lord of glory.*

The Holy Spirit will use divinely-empowered experiences to replace those lies with the Truth.

> *But as it is written:*
> *"Eye has not seen, nor ear heard,*
> *Nor have entered into the heart of man*

*The things which God has prepared
for those who love Him"* [Isaiah 64:4]

*But God has revealed them to us through His Spirit. For the Spirit
searches all things, yes, the deep things of God. For what man knows
the things of a man except the spirit of the man which is in him?
Even so no one knows the things of God except the Spirit of God.
Now we have received, not the spirit of the world, but the Spirit who
is from God, that we might know the things that have been freely
given to us by God.*

*These things we also speak, not in words which man's wisdom teaches
but which the Holy Spirit teaches, comparing spiritual things with
spiritual. But the natural man does not receive the things of the
Spirit of God, for they are foolishness to him; nor can he know them,
because they are spiritually discerned. But he who is spiritual judges
all things, yet he himself is rightly judged by no one. For "who has
known the mind of the Lord that he may instruct Him?"
But we have the mind of Christ.*

1 Corinthians 2:4-16

Paul is dealing with the Corinthians about a distorted version of wisdom, a celebrated Greek notion of elitism that they are confusing with the gifts of the Spirit in their midst. They are experiencing an abundance of inspired "utterances and knowledge" (1 Cor. 1:6-7) but confusing it with a pagan notion that is dividing God's Spirit-people (*pneumatikoi*) rather than bringing them to wholeness in diversity. He reasserts that the Gospel he preaches is actually the true wisdom from God for a people to whom the Spirit has revealed what God has accomplished in Christ (i.e., bringing them out of darkness into light, from orphans to sons). The rulers of this age (including principalities and powers) indeed can't comprehend it because they are not born of the Spirit.

Something Drastic Has Changed

Note carefully how Paul, immediately after addressing Greek philosophical notions, quotes from the Older Covenant, not just to

25

include the Jewish believers in the Corinthian church, but also to contrast a significant difference between the Older Covenant and the New. Paul quotes Isaiah 64:4:

> *Eye has not seen, neither has ear heard what God has prepared*
> *for those who love Him.*
>
> 1 Corinthians 2:9

If Paul stopped there, it would appear that he was reinforcing the Old Testament reality of a disconnect between the human spirit and God's Spirit, but something has changed. There is a new reality. The Spirit has come by the new birth (John 20:22) and has been poured out (Acts 2:1-4) to fulfill what Jesus had said:

> *He* [the Spirit] *dwells with you and will be in you.*
>
> John 14:17

In the Old Testament, we couldn't see with our spiritual eyes or hear with our spiritual ears. We were "dead" in our trespasses and sins. Our hearts were darkened, and we were alien to the Life of God. The Old Testament saints couldn't speak God's language—if you will—because they didn't have His Spirit in their spirits. Paul says, however, "That was then, but this is now." Note verse 10:

> *But God has revealed them to us through His Spirit.*
>
> 1 Corinthians 2:10

What is the "them" that has now been revealed to us who are Spirit-people? "Them" is referring to the things God has prepared for those who love Him. I know it is terrible grammar, but I want to say it this way so it will stick sideways in your mind: God has moved His Spirit into your spirit so He can reveal to you "them things" that He has prepared for you, "them things" which have in times past been hidden from the eyes of our heart but are now revealed by the Spirit. "Them things" are the plans and purpose of God for His sons and daughters. "Them

In the Old Testament, we couldn't see with our spiritual eyes or hear with our spiritual ears. We were "dead" in our trespasses and sins.

things" are the unimaginable realities in which we will share as "heirs of God and joint heirs with Jesus Christ" (Rom. 8:17).

God Is Not Hiding, But Revealing to You

Two things are important here from verse 10. **First, God is not hiding or concealing from you what He has planned for you.** He is *revealing* these things to you by His Spirit which He has put in you. (I know, we have been told all our lives, "You never can tell what God is going to do," but that was also a lie). God is a relational God. He loves partnership. He loves telling His kids what He has planned for them!

Think about Jesus' story of the Prodigal Son. The story is really not so much about the son, as it is a revealing of the Father's heart toward His children. The son comes back, and the father is overjoyed! The father in Jesus' story didn't whisper to the servants to keep the prodigal from hearing, "Shhh … don't tell anyone, but go kill the fatted calf, get the robe, the sandals, the ring … but let's not tell him that we are welcoming him home. He may get the wrong idea. He may actually believe that I want him here. Better yet, let's hide the party and see if he can figure it out." No! He shouted it: "We're going to have a party! My son who was dead is alive again and has come back home!" See this loving, happy, laughing, dancing God who likes to shower His children with His goodness!

The Father wants to reveal to you the things He has prepared for you— His plans and purposes for your life. Does He do that all at once? No, He takes time. Otherwise we wouldn't be able to handle the scope of His goodness. Someone said, "Time is what God made so that life wouldn't happen to us all at once." Spiritual hunger has a lot to do with timing, the how and when He discloses.

Second, He is communicating to us, but not primarily to our minds. God is not a mind but a spirit (John 4:24), and He has put His Spirit in our spirits to commune and communicate with us Spirit-to-spirit.

For as many as are led by the Spirit of God, these are sons of God.
Romans 8:14

This revelation will shift many things for you. How often the enemy lies to you saying everyone hears God except you. You cry, "God, why can't I hear Your voice?" The reality is He is not speaking to your mind; He is speaking to your spirit by the Holy Spirit. Our expectation is misdirected. Many believers have never located their spirit-man because they don't pray in the Spirit, sing in the Spirit, or worship out of their spirit. Paul states that when we pray in an unknown tongue, the Spirit within us prays (1 Cor. 14:14). We will talk more about this in a later chapter, but the more you allow the Holy Spirit to pray, sing, and worship through your spirit, the more you will learn to distinguish the voice of your mind from the voice of your spirit and realize that God is indeed, always speaking (Matt. 4:4).

The Psalmist provides the foretaste of what was to come—rivers of knowing by the Holy Spirit in our spirits—saying:

> *Deep waters call out to what is deeper still;*
> *at the roar of your waterfalls*
> *all your breakers and your waves swirled over me.*
> *By day the Lord will command his gracious love,*
> *and by night his song is with me—*
> *a prayer to the God of my life.*
> Psalm 42:7-8 (ISV)

I want you to see that we have been breathing the air of the Enlightenment (which values a scientific approach to reality by empirical data and reason) for so long, that we don't realize we have tried to force God to speak and work on our terms. We insist that we won't believe it unless we can analyze the hard data of our five senses with our finite minds, even subjecting the Bible to mental criteria that suffocates the supernatural realities of a spiritual world which preceded the natural one. But God is still speaking, and He is inviting us into the conversation by His Spirit. In the following chapter we will look at how the indwelling Holy Spirit synchronizes our spirits to the things of God in such a way that we can begin to "get up to speed" with what God is doing in us, for us, and through us. It's an inside job.

What Have We Said?

Mephibosheth provides the prototypical story of the orphan spirit. Although he was born to be raised in the King's Palace, he believes lies both about the King and about himself, thereby living a life of squalor and pain. His life, however, begins to change once the King's servant brings him home.

Willpower is insufficient to replace the lies that we have believed about God and ourselves. Information has little power to bring lasting change. We need the Spirit of God.

Paul had a change of strategy. He realized that transformation couldn't come by the eloquence of man's wisdom. Instead, the demonstration of the Spirit's power is essential for lasting change.

What couldn't be seen, heard or spiritually perceived in the Old Testament is now available because the Spirit has come and made His home in the hearts of believers, teaching us all things. Deep calls unto deep.

The good news is that God is not hiding from us His will and purposes. He is revealing them to us by His Spirit. Sons and daughters of God are led by the Spirit into a new world of God's inheritance.

PRAYER

Abba, I see that I have been like Mephibosheth in many ways. I have believed lies about who You are and what You have intended for me. I have lived in a wasteland and somehow believed that was Your plan for my life. I repent of any judgments, animosity, or resentment toward You. Thank you for sending Your servant, the Holy Spirit, to lead me back to the King's Palace. Thank you for the unsearchable riches, the grand inheritance You have reserved for all who are in Jesus. My mind can't comprehend it, but you are making it real to my spirit by the Holy Spirit. Thank You, Holy Spirit, that now my spiritual eyes can see, and my spiritual ears are beginning to hear about all the Father has prepared for me through the Son, my elder Brother, Jesus. Amen.

GROUP DISCUSSION

1. In what ways is Mephibosheth's story all of humanity's story? How do you personally relate to it?

2. Why isn't willpower and mental study (education) enough to solve our problems or bring lasting transformation?

3. Why did Paul come to Corinth saying (paraphrased), "I don't want to know anything except Jesus Christ and Him crucified. My preaching was not just about persuasive words, but the demonstration of the Spirit's power"?

4. According to 1 Corinthians 2:9-10, how can we have "ears that hear and eyes that see" in ways that the Old Testament saints could not have?

Two

An Inside Job

Christ is not the abstract, but the concrete.
If God is love, Christ is love for this one person, this one place,
this one time-bound and time-ravaged self.
— Christian Wimam

Would you like to see inside the Trinity—get a peek at how Father, Son and Holy Spirit relate? Paul, by his abundance of revelations, grants us insight into the internal workings of the Trinity when he tells us how God reveals these things to us by the Holy Spirit. He says:

> *For the Spirit searches all things, yes, the deep things of God.*
> 1 Corinthians 2:10

The Amplified Version renders it like this:

> *The Spirit searches all things* [diligently], *even* [sounding and measuring] *the* [profound] *depths of God* [the divine counsels and things far beyond human understanding].
> 1 Corinthians 2:10 (AMP)

The Message paraphrases it as:

> *The Spirit, not content to flit around on the surface, dives into the depths of God, and brings out what God planned all along.*
> 1 Corinthians 2:10 (MSG)

Here we are swimming in water too deep for our minds to try to understand how the Spirit of God goes in and searches out the depths of the Father's purposes for each of His children. It is a staggering thought. The fact that our God would *want* to know and be known by us in such a way is even more glorious! Jesus described the same relational interaction (knowing), when He said:

> [The Holy Spirit] *will not speak on His own authority, but whatever He hears He will speak; and He will tell you things to come ... He will take of what is Mine and declare it to you. All things that the Father has are Mine. Therefore I said that [the Spirit] will take of Mine and declare it to you.*
>
> John 16:13-15

Into the Conversation of the Trinity

It is easy to miss the significance of this. If our orphan thinking, especially if it's shrouded in religious notions of a rule-keeping, judgmental God, sees holiness as perfectionism and performance rather than wholeness in relationship, then it's difficult to grasp that we have been invited into the ongoing conversation of the Trinity. Listen to Jesus' words:

> *No longer do I call you servants, for a servant does not know what his master is doing; but I have called you friends, for all things that I heard from My Father I have made known to you.*
>
> John 15:15

From Jesus' perspective, we are included in the ongoing conversation of the Trinity. The work of redemption is an inside job, inside the Holiest of Holies, the inner circle of the inner circle. The Father is constantly revealing His heart, plans, and purposes to Jesus, and it's only natural that Jesus, as the Head of the Church, would want and need the Father's plans and purposes for His disciples. Jesus then shares those things with the Spirit, who in turn reveals them to us in an ongoing dynamic dance of joyful, overflowing knowing. This is the prodigal son's father shouting out to the servants, "Get the ring, the robe, the sandals! I have big plans! And, yes, the fattest calf too! Big plans!"

Hear Jesus say it again:

> *When He, the Spirit of truth, has come, He will guide you into all truth; for He will not speak on His own authority, but whatever He hears He will speak; and He will tell you things to come. He will glorify Me, for He will take of what is Mine and declare it to you. All things that the Father has are*

Mine. Therefore I said that He will take of Mine and declare it to you.

John 16:13-15

What is prayer if it is not being invited into the conversation of the Trinity?

You and I have been baptized—brought into the realm of the Father, Son and Holy Spirit. It is more than our minds can comprehend, but we have been caught up into the life of the Triune God. The Old Testament way of saying this, as described in the previous chapter, is, "Mephibosheth, you have a place at my table, and you will eat my food, dine with me, and have all that I have."

What is prayer if it is not being invited into the conversation of the Trinity? Do you see God as so aloof and far off that prayer is nothing more than depositing a piece of paper in a "Leave Your Comments" box? Is prayer only submitting your request and then waiting patiently to see if something happens, or does it include the sweet communion of intimacy, hearing one another's voice, sharing dreams and hopes? We will examine this part of the Triune conversation in Chapter 8, *Sonship Implications on Prayer*.

To be certain that we don't miss this, allow me to bullet point what we have just said:

- The Holy Spirit goes to the Father (in Triune fellowship) and receives the Father's plans and purposes for you, His child (1 Cor. 2:10).

- Jesus also receives the plans and purposes of the Father directly (in Triune fellowship) and shares those with the Holy Spirit, so the Holy Spirit can share them with you (John 16:13-15).

- Jesus no longer calls us servants, but friends, specifically because He wants to declare to us (in Triune fellowship) what the Father is saying about us and to us (John 15:15).

This is why worship and prayer are so critical to the life of the believer and the Church corporately. It is in the place of His Presence that we are pouring our hearts out as participants in the Triune conversation of praise, adoration, intimacy, intercession, and petition. It's an engagement with the Trinity because we are coming directly to the Father, through the Son, by the Spirit (John 16:23). In that place of presence, we hear His voice

It's not the mind of man ... it is the spirit of a man that knows the man. and, to our surprise, the Father is speaking to us more about who we are as His sons and daughters (e.g. "this is My beloved son, in whom I am well pleased") than giving directives or issuing commands and corrections. With God, you will find out it is always more about the "who" than the "what" or "when."

Coming back to 1 Corinthians 2, Paul underscores what should be well understood:

For what man knows the things of a man except the spirit of the man which is in him? Even so no one knows the things of God except the Spirit of God.
1 Corinthians 2:11

Notice that he puts no confidence in the flesh and no confidence in the mind, though Paul would have consistently had the highest IQ in any room he was in. It's not the mind of man, it's not the physical strength of man, it is the spirit of a man that knows the man. In the same way (since we are made in God's image and after His design), no one comprehends God by the power of his mind or just by the physical universe—though we can make inferences by observing what He has made.

In 1 Corinthians 2:12 Paul is connecting the dots. He says that since God's Spirit really knows God, and man's spirit is the part of man that really knows the man, God has put His Spirit in the hearts of His Spirit-people (*pneumatikoi*)[8] in order for them to know the things of God! God's Spirit teaches man's spirit about God. We can know God, but this knowing and communication is carried out Spirit-to-spirit.

Synchronizing My Spirit to God's Spirit

Paul continues his discourse and takes the conversation into another orbit. He tells us how God brings man into His very own life, into the circle of the Triune life of Father, Son, and Holy Spirit.

These things we also speak, not in words which man's wisdom teaches but which the Holy Spirit teaches, comparing spiritual things with spiritual.
1 Corinthians 2:13

This begs the question, "How does the Holy Spirit teach me in my spirit? How does the Holy Spirit take the things the Father has given to Jesus, and download those spiritual realities into my spirit and your spirit?" This is the *Abba Formation*.

Paul uses a particularly insightful word here and in 2 Corinthians 10:12. The word is *sygkrinō* and it is usually translated *"to compare."* This is a conjugated form of the compound word, *synkrinō*. *Syn* means "with," and *krinō* means "to sunder so as to judge or assess."[9] We can illustrate it with an avocado.

Think about slicing an avocado in two pieces so that what is on the inside of both halves can be viewed and compared, judged and assessed. The avocado is a great illustration because once opened, that huge seed is nestled in one half while the other half has a nice empty cavity where the seed used to be. Can you visualize it?

Using this as a metaphor, we can say that one side represents God, with the seed representing the Spirit of God at the center. The other half is man, made in God's image but without the Spirit. There is that large hollow void where the seed used to be. Now bring the two halves together again and let that big seed shift from one half to the other. This illustrates Paul's idea that God sends His Spirit into our hearts. On a physical level, the seed of the avocado is what keeps its flesh from decaying. This is, of course, yet another metaphor of the work of the Holy Spirit in our lives. What concerns us at this point, however, is how the Holy Spirit synchronizes us with God's plans and purposes for us. Paul says:

> *We have received ... the Spirit who is from God, that we might know the things that have been freely given to us by God.*
> 1 Corinthians 2:12

A curious person opens up the avocado to see inside in order to judge whether the two halves are alike or dissimilar (*synkrinō*). In 1 Corinthians 2, the comparison is between God's Spirit and man's spirit—what God knows about the man compared to what man knows about the man. The Spirit of God, however, is the one taking inventory of what is in God's thoughts and to what degree that is missing from the man's inner thoughts. In the same process, the Spirit of God begins to download whatever is in God's heart that is missing from the man's heart. Another way to say this, closer to Paul's way, is that man's deepest levels of knowing, thinking, and believing (longings, visions, dreams and desires) are being synchronized (*sygkrinō*) with God's thoughts, plans and purposes (longings, visions, dreams and desires for the man).

Please don't miss this. Paul is telling us that the ongoing work of the Holy Spirit in you is to synchronize your spirit (your knowing, believing, will and desires) with God's thoughts, plans and purposes for you. The Holy Spirit is the active agent—He is doing the synchronizing in you. He is changing and transforming the knowing, the "want-tos," the understanding of God's plans and purposes for you. This is not about your wrestling your will to the ground and forcing yourself to keep certain laws or making yourself do things you don't want to do. That is outside-in living. Life in the Spirit is inside-out. Paul says it like this to the Philippians:

> *For it is* [not your strength, but it is] *God who is effectively at work in you, both to will and to work* [that is, strengthening, energizing, and <u>creating in you</u> the longing and the ability to fulfill your purpose] *for His good pleasure.*
> Philippians 2:13 (AMP)

When you open up and compare (*sygkrinō*) what the Spirit of God is seeing in God and what He is doing in believers, it can be summed up like this: the Spirit of God is taking the thoughts, plans and purposes of God, downloading those into you in such a way that they strengthen, energize and create in you the longing and ability to fulfill your purpose and the Father's good pleasure. The Spirit of God is energizing sons to fulfill the Father's unfinished business of filling the whole earth with His glory and bringing many sons to that glory!

The Transmission of the Spirit

Here's a modern parable or parallel. If you drive a vehicle with an automatic transmission, this synchronizing process is going on all the time. It's automatic. The engine is creating thousands of revolutions per minute, but that power must slowly and gently be transferred to the wheels on your car to make it move. The connecting mechanism between that powerful engine and the wheels is a drive shaft and a transmission, which is a series of small gears with teeth that interlock. As the vehicle moves from one size cog to the next, it allows the axle and wheels to slowly catch up to speed with the speed of the engine. As you can imagine, there is a lot of stress and heat being generated through these gears so a transmission fluid—a special kind of oil—bathes these gears constantly. It is the fluid in the transmission that prevents all the moving parts from overheating. It is also the fluid circulating over a complicated system of gears which makes that transfer of power from engine to axle a fairly unconscious

By the Holy Spirit, God can synchronize you to His plans and purposes and bring you "up to speed" on what He wants to do in your life.

process for the driver. If you drive an automatic transmission (i.e., you are not shifting gears by hand), you may not even feel the car shifting through each gear and back down again. That's how our life in the Spirit is to be: *synchronized* with God in such a way that "the yoke is easy, and the burden is light" (Matt. 11:30).

Of course, Paul couldn't have had a vehicle in mind, but he understood that the Holy Spirit in the heart of the believer makes it possible for an infinite, all-powerful God to download measures of His infinite knowledge and power in such a way that it would not overheat us with the glory of God. Let's say it another way: *By the Holy Spirit, God can synchronize you to His plans and purposes and bring you "up to speed" on what He wants to do in your life*, thereby getting you in alignment with His plans. Just as you shift through a series of gears over and over on a simple drive to the grocery store, the Holy Spirit is recalculating over and over, with every thought and decision you make, to keep you synchronized to the will of God.[10] God's people are empowered to move at a totally different speed so that the world around us says, "How did you do that?" "How did you solve that problem, create that invention, design that architectural wonder, or write that kind of song?" Do you see that the Church should be leading the way in every enterprise and creation by the indwelling genius of the Holy Spirit?

Paul applies this synchronizing idea to his immediate problem. On one hand, Judaizers were trying to lure Gentile believers into Old Testament regulations. On the other, Gnostics were teaching lasciviousness—that because of God's grace we can sin all we want. Paul wants to show both sides that the indwelling Spirit of the New Covenant is how God's people fulfill the whole Law. The Gospel is no longer a sin-management program, building fences around our behaviors so we don't "act out." Neither does Paul prescribe layers of accountability groups to ensure external controls, though relationships play a key role in ongoing Spirit-fullness (Col. 2:20-22).

I am contending for the abiding presence of the Spirit upon my life so that I stay tender and responsive in my heart. The New Covenant is not about trying to maintain a rigid will against wrong thoughts and evil desires. This only makes us more religious, closed-minded and judgmental. No. God has put His Spirit inside us, changing us from the inside, *synchronizing* our heart with His so that the very thing He wants is now what we want. My "want-tos" catch up to speed with His "want-tos." My desires are constantly being synchronized to His by the Holy Spirit (Phil. 2:13). This means that I am contending from a position of passionate desire and internal motivation by the Spirit, not against my will, or even against the devil. I am contending for the abiding presence of the Spirit upon my life so that I stay tender and responsive in my heart to the gentle whispers, the words the Spirit uses to keep me moving at the Father's pace for me. This is transformation. This is the *Abba Formation*.

God has moved into His people, making us (the Church) a people of the S/spirit (*pneumatikoi*).[11] (The unusual notation of S/spirit throughout the book is used to denote the Holy Spirit in our human spirit). Paul is referring to the people of the S/spirit when he says that life in the Spirit has fulfilled the law (Rom. 8:4). Paul says plainly that if we are filled with the overflow of the Spirit's life in us (i.e., the "fruit of the Spirit"), we will not be breaking the laws of God (Gal. 5:22), not because we learn neat mind tricks to keep ourselves in check, but because our desires are being transformed.

The begging question is, how do we make sure the "fluid levels" stay full in our spiritual transmission so that (1) the transformational work of the Holy Spirit is a continuous and practically unnoticeable lifelong process, and (2) we are not overheating or cooling to the extremes? We will certainly take up the "how to" questions in later chapters, but for now let's apply the synchronizing reality in yet another way.

Synchronizing Spirit, Soul and Body

Not only does the Holy Spirit compound truths to our spirits and synchronize our spirits to the will and ways of God, but He brings us to wholeness so that what has been fractured and disintegrated between our spirits, soul and body is brought into a process of reintegration and wholeness. We are designed to be a wholeness, an integrated three-and-oneness the same way Father, Son and Spirit are three-and-one.

Notice how Paul prays for the Thessalonians:

Now may the God of peace Himself sanctify you completely;
and may your whole spirit, soul, and body be preserved blameless
at the coming of our Lord Jesus Christ. He who calls you is faithful,
who also will do it.

1 Thessalonians 5:23-24

1. Synchronized in spirit (*pneuma*). Paul makes it clear that the Holy Spirit's concern is for our whole sanctification (spirit, soul, and body). It starts in the spirit and affects the soul and the body. Interestingly, in an earlier verse Paul says:

Do not quench the Spirit.

1 Thessalonians 5:19

It is the Holy Spirit who prays when we pray in the S/spirit, sings when we sing with the S/spirit, or gives thanks through us to the Father (1 Cor. 14:14-16). When I am filled with the Spirit, my spirit is filled with God's love (Rom. 5:5); I have "unspeakable joy" and am filled with God's glory even in times of difficulty (1 Pet. 1:8), and I can strengthen myself in faith by releasing prayer by the Spirit in my spirit (Jude 20).

2. Synchronized in soul (*psuche*—mind, will and emotions). The soul is where much of the long-term damage is felt even after someone comes to Christ. When a person is born again by receiving the redemptive work of Christ, there is an instantaneous work of regeneration in his spirit:

Therefore, if anyone is in Christ, he is a new creation; old things [the spiritual nature of sin and death] *have passed away; behold, all things* [in the spirit of a man] *have become new.*

2 Corinthians 5:17

The debris of our orphan ways, however, lingers in the soul through memories, appetites, strongholds, orphan thinking and personal habits. Much like soldiers who have been in battle have to work through Post

Traumatic Stress Disorder (PTSD), believers can have a soul that is broken, wounded, and shell-shocked. Although our spirits experience an immediate regeneration when we are born of the Spirit, our minds, will and emotions must be submitted to a restoration process that takes time. Paul speaks about this process:

> *Be renewed in the spirit* [attitudes] *of your mind.*
>
> Ephesians 4:23

> *Do not be conformed to this world, but be transformed* [metamorphoō] *by the renewing of you mind.*
>
> Romans 12:2

The metamorphosis Paul is referring to is not primarily a mental exercise as though a person can renew his or her own mind by diligent effort. It is a work of the Spirit from within. The spirit (*pneuma*) is that which has its ultimate impact upon the mind. The butterfly doesn't metamorphose from caterpillar state by self-effort. It is in its nature to transform through a cocoon state; then the wings take shape. The reality of the butterfly is programmed into the nature of the caterpillar long before it spins a cocoon.

The renewing of the mind is a work of the Spirit, not a mental self-exercise. The design and fullness of a person spring up like fountains from the spirit of the person, by the work of the Holy Spirit. To use the car metaphor, the renewing of the mind is just another shift of the automatic transmission—the mind catching up to what the heart already knows in God. There is an emotional element to the synchronization. This can be seen in the fruit of the spirit (love, joy, peace, etc.), so it is not only the realm of understanding or insight, but the realm of feeling. Hurts are healed, wounds are made whole, and sensitive emotions are made strong again.

Think about the numerous times we see Jesus being "moved with compassion." Standing before Lazarus' tomb, Jesus wept. He was moved with compassion. Compassion is an emotion that comes from the deepest place, from spirit to soul. It is the Spirit of God that releases the love of God in our hearts—sheds abroad, floods us (Rom. 5:5)—to such an overflowing dimension, until our souls catch the overflow and we feel it in our

The renewing of the mind is a work of the Spirit, not a mental self-exercise.

emotions. This is the spirit and soul of a person being synchronized by the Spirit of God.

How It Looks in Real Life

While writing this book, a pastor friend of mine told me about a grueling experience he had due to identity theft. Because of what someone else did with his personal information, my friend had a warrant issued for his arrest. He had to make multiple trips to the county courthouse to appeal the mistake and began to experience anxiety attacks. Sitting in his car in the courthouse parking lot after one of these attacks, he said, "Lord, what is this? I've never had this problem before." Then the Lord simply asked him if he could imagine what it would be like to feel this anxiety while being incarcerated with no one to appeal to for help. In that instant he remembered a lady in his church whose husband was serving a lengthy sentence in federal prison because of false accusations. The pastor felt prompted to commit to pray for that husband, and had a compassion come upon him for this man and his wife who hadn't seen her husband in a couple of years. Within a fairly short time, the prisoner was moved from a California prison back to his home state where he was able to see his wife regularly.

What happened? In that *Abba Cry* to God, this pastor's soul was synchronized by God's Spirit with his own spirit, and he was moved by the Holy Spirit to get his eyes on someone else who was in a worse situation than his own. Rather than groveling in self-pity, he caught up to speed with what was on God's heart. He became an intercessor for that couple until something changed. Please note: here is one of the primary gauges on the dashboard of your sonship. The spirit of sonship will move you to shift your focus from you to others. As we will see later, that's how the son engages in the Father's business.

In the early years of my first pastorate, I had an elderly man stand up in a public meeting and say some pretty rough things about me. (I'm sure I deserved the criticism as I was still in my twenties, pastoring people who were three times my age. I still pray for those folks who put up with my youthful arrogance and ambition.) At first, there was a grace upon me; I didn't feel hurt by his accusations. After a few days, though, the man's words began to fester in my soul and I could feel unforgiveness rising

Rather than groveling in self-pity, he caught up to speed with what was on God's heart.

in me. In the process of crying out to God for help, He showed me how to go beyond praying "the forgiveness prayer" and begin to bless the man. Twice a day I prayed for him, speaking blessing over his life. It felt unnatural at first, but within a couple of weeks I was so healed and transformed in my emotions that one day, while driving by his house, I was overcome with compassion for him, pulled into his driveway and knocked on his door to share this feeling with him. We were reconciled that day because the Holy Spirit synchronized my soul with my spirit—and with the heart of God for that man.

As you lean into spiritual language (praying in an unknown tongue), you make room for the Holy Spirit to pray, sing, and worship through your spirit. You will find your mind, will and emotions being progressively transformed. This is a lifetime process of sanctification which starts in our spirits, by the Holy Spirit, and impacts the renewing of the soul (mind, will and emotions). This process can literally change your neurological patterns and physiological responses by turning "on" or "off" certain DNA genes that energize or minimize the chemical responses that promote desires, thoughts, and habits. In Chapter 4 we will discuss the neuroscience of Epigenetics and how the sins which are passed down to the third and fourth generations (spiritually, emotionally and genetically) can be transformed by life in the Spirit. Suffice it to say, it's one thing to try to use willpower to keep one's sin management systems in place, and a far different thing to have the power of sin uprooted altogether. There is a verifiable link between being renewed in the "spirit of your mind" and "training your senses (physical appetites) to discern good from evil" (Heb. 5:14). We will look more closely at the way science is confirming Scripture via the study of genetics shortly, but the ultimate conclusion of all transformation is living out our new life in God, even to the point of our physical body being empowered by the Spirit.

3. Synchronized in the Body (*soma*). I have said that the *Abba Cry*, which starts most fundamentally in our spirit man by the Holy Spirit, is about being convinced and convicted by the Holy Spirit that we are sons of God. The same Spirit that raised Jesus from the dead, the Holy Spirit, quickens our mortal bodies with that same resurrection life (Rom. 8:11). Yes, though the context of that verse would apply to the ultimate resurrection of the body, the principle is the same.

The Holy Spirit is the down payment of the consummated kingdom of God where these mortal bodies will put on immortality and these corruptible bodies will put on incorruption (1 Cor. 15:53). The same Holy Spirit who anointed Jesus of Nazareth—who went about healing all that were sick (Acts 10:38)—is still healing sick bodies today. The Triune God paid the same price for your physical healing as He did your mental wholeness and your spiritual regeneration (Isa. 53:3-5). This synchronization of body with soul and spirit is not just about physical healing, though it is very much that. It also affects how this body can be used as a weapon for either righteousness or wickedness. The work of the Spirit by the *Abba Cry* in your spirit is to see you walking in wholeness—spirit, soul and body—as a son of God. This means that we are not praising God with our mouths on Sunday and sinning with our eyes or bodies on Monday.

Paul dealt with this orphan thinking when he told the Roman believers:

> *Now what is our response to be? Shall we sin to our heart's content*
> *and see how far we can exploit the grace of God?*
> *What a ghastly thought! We, who have died to sin—*
> *how could we live in sin a moment longer?*
> Romans 6:1-2 (JBP)

Overcoming Temptation by the Spirit

The Lord taught me a powerful lesson about how to deal with temptations that warred as passions in my body. In my early twenties I was experiencing plenty of it! He used Romans, chapter 6, to show me that I could partner with the Holy Spirit in the area of fleshly temptation by putting His Word in my mouth as both a two-edged sword and a shield of faith against the fiery darts of the enemy (Eph. 6:16-17). He said, "Put My word in your mouth, and in so doing, reckon your body as dead to sin." That was Romans 6 language.

I wrote all of Romans 6 on index cards and kept them in my back pocket. I meditated on those verses several times a day, and any time I would feel a stirring of temptation in my desires I would pull those cards out and begin to declare the scriptures out loud (audible is physical). I would begin with, "What shall I say to this sin?" Then I would name my particular temptation everywhere the word *sin* came up in the chapter. I spoke the Word out loud in first person, reckoning (applying, accounting) Christ's death, burial and resurrection as my own (Gal. 2:20).

What I discovered changed my life. I found that whenever I spoke that assigned Word in faith, God's Spirit would come upon me, even physically. I discovered that the Holy Spirit would literally drive that craving out of my body, replacing the temptation with praise. By partnering with the Holy Spirit, I had His power to resist temptation. Paul says:

> *And do not present your members as instruments* [hoplon—weapons] *of unrighteousness to sin, but present yourselves to God as being alive from the dead, and your members as instruments* [weapons] *of righteousness to God. For sin shall not have dominion over you, for you are not under law but under grace.*
>
> Romans 6: 13-14

The Holy Spirit will help you synchronize your body to the plans, purposes, and power of God. Sin shall not have dominion over you. I discovered the link between my spirit and my mouth. I discovered that there is a language of sonship, an *Abba Cry* that synchronizes your spirit, soul and body to the things of God.

Paul said that it was God at work within him both to will and to do of His good pleasure (Phil. 2:13). He labored more abundantly than all others because of the grace of God working within him, the precious Gift of the Holy Spirit.

A Lifetime of Synchronizing and "Recalculating"

Present yourselves to God as being alive from the dead, and your members as instruments [weapons] of righteousness.

As we said earlier, the *Abba Cry* is a lifelong cry to God as our Heavenly Father that is not to be outgrown, but rather to be grown into. This Spirit of adoption is at work in every believer, continually synchronizing our inner man and our desires to God's will and purpose for us. We have seen that the Holy Spirit is tenaciously searching out the heart of God, gathering the "deep things of God"—His plans and purposes for your life—and downloading those into your own spirit. In other words, the Holy Spirit is recalibrating and recalculating your self-understanding based upon what God has always purposed for you. Think about this. God says:

> *For I know the thoughts that I think toward you, says the Lord,*
> *thoughts of peace and not of evil, to give you a future and a hope.*
> Jeremiah 29:11

The Holy Spirit is assigned to "take those thoughts of Mine and give them to you" (John 16:15). When you and I put our lives in His hands, invite Him to take over and say, "Your kingdom come, Your will be done in my life," then the Holy Spirit can work with our prayer to recalibrate our thoughts and desires to the Father's good pleasure. He actually synchronizes our "want-tos" to align with His "want-tos" for us. Much like the GPS system in your car, when you miss your turn or get on the wrong road that voice will say, "recalculating, recalculating." As you and I continually surrender our lives to the Lord, the Spirit of adoption recalculates the path of our feet toward the Father's good pleasure. For the most part, His work often goes unannounced and unnoticed in us. He causes new ideas and different kinds of thoughts to bubble up from our spirits to our minds. We have a new possibility arise in our minds that we had not considered before. We wake up in the morning with an urge to do something or to talk to someone we haven't considered before. God is reordering our steps to His.

The enemy wants to keep you paralyzed by self-conscious thoughts, "Am I doing the will of God?" "Is this what I am supposed to be doing?" "God, what is Your will for my life?" But, you can enter into a new kind of rest. You can know that "they that are led by the Spirit of God are the sons of God" (Rom. 8:14). You will know what you need to know when you need to know it. You will have what you need to have when you need to have it. You are a son of God and nothing happens to sons by accident. You don't have to live in the fear of missing God's will. As you keep your heart open before Him, you rest in the fact that the Holy Spirit is constantly working beneath the surface of your awareness to constantly synchronize your spirit to the Father.

Ponder this:

> *No more shall every man teach his neighbor,*
> *and every man his brother, saying, "Know the Lord,"*

You are being restored, synchronized, and calibrated to the life of heaven.

for they [my sons] *all shall know Me, from the least of them to the greatest of them, says the Lord. For I will forgive their iniquity, and their sin I will remember no more.*

Jeremiah 31:34

With the Holy Spirit synchronizing your heart to the Father's by the *Abba Cry* (a revelation of sonship), you are being restored, synchronized, and calibrated to the life of heaven. You are coming to the place where you have nothing to fear, nothing to prove, nothing to hide, and nothing to lose. You can be who He has made you to be, and it is good. You can release heaven here in the earth with confidence.

What Have We Said?

Our spiritual maturity is not a product of our own efforts; it's an "inside job" in which the Holy Spirit downloads the will and plan of God in our spirits.

We have been invited into the ongoing conversation of the Trinity— with both the Spirit and Son sharing with us what the Father is saying about us. Our prayers and worship are welcome in the conversation.

In 1 Corinthians 2 Paul uses the idea of synchronization to explain how the Holy Spirit gets us "up to speed" with God's will and plan.

Two illustrations for this *Abba Formation* process are the comparing of two halves of an avocado, and the transmission of an automobile (releasing the power of the engine slowly to the rear axle).

The Holy Spirit not only works to synchronize our hearts to God's heart but also to synchronize every believer's spirit, soul, and body into an integrated wholeness.

Prayer:

Wow, God! You are creating and energizing me in my spirit, by Your Holy Spirit, to please You in every way. You have not put the burden upon me to make myself whole or spiritual. I simply invite You to fill me more. I want to abide more and more in Your presence. I invite

You to pour more of the oil of gladness into my life so You "catch me up" to all that You want to do in my life. I will not worry about missing Your will—I will simply abide in Your presence. Holy Spirit, pray through me, sing through me, worship through me any way and every way that You wish. Thank you, Father, for inviting me into the conversation of Your plans and purposes, by the grace of Jesus, and the communion of the Spirit. Amen.

GROUP DISCUSSION

1. How does the "inside-out" life contrast to the "outside-in" life?

2. In what way does an avocado cut in half illustrate the Spirit's synchronization (*sunkrinō*) between God's heart and our own?

3. In what way does the transmission of a car illustrate how the Holy Spirit works transformation in a believer's life?

4. In what way does staying full of the Spirit impact the need to know the will of God or the concern to be in God's will?

5. What other thought stood out to you that you would like to talk about?

Three

Restored to Childlikeness

The great beauty of childlikeness is the absence of self-consciousness.
— Andrew Murray

The *Abba Cry* Is Child Language

In the previous chapter we took a deep dive to see how the Holy Spirit, who dwells in our spirits, searches out the deep things of God. Because the Holy Spirit is God and one with the Father and the Son, He has ready access to both our spirits and God's, and He synchronizes our spirits to the Father's good will and purpose for us. But do we have any idea what that might look like? Is there a pattern or a template from which He might be working? Is there a "before-and-after picture," a blueprint He would use that we can identify? What are we being set free from and to? What does that look like? Did Jesus give us any clues?

Our primary clue in Scripture comes from both Jesus and the Apostle Paul. As we discussed in *The Abba Factor* and *The Abba Foundation*, Jesus first gives us a glimpse of another way of living when the disciples ask Him to teach them to pray. He said:

> *In this manner, therefore, pray:*
> *Our Father in heaven,*
> *Hallowed be Your name.*
>
> Matthew 6:9

This was a watershed moment in human history—the first documented incident in which humanity had been invited into a new kind of relationship with God. It was certainly new for the Jewish people, who wouldn't dare refer to Almighty God using the Aramaic toddler term for "Daddy." Nevertheless Paul, by revelation, lays hold of the term in a significant way. In his letters to both the Romans and the Galatians, he asserts that we have been brought into a never-before imagined relationship of Father to sons/

daughters, and that this adoption is consummated by an ongoing internal transformation via a recalibrating cry from our spirits by the Holy Spirit, "*Abba*, Father!"[12]

The *Abba* references give us a clue as to what God is up to. He is restoring us to a place of trust, intimacy, and interdependence that is only known in childlikeness. He is challenging our "grown-up" ways of analytical either-or dualism, the knowledge of good and evil, and the spirit of independence. Once we see that childlikeness is a way of being, it brings other things Jesus said into focus. For example, what did Jesus mean when He said, "Unless you become like (turn back to) a child you won't enter the kingdom"? If it is about childlikeness, what practical steps can I take to shed my grown-up clothes?

Being Restored to Childlikeness

I've been told the Japanese have a saying they use when an outsider comes in among them. They say, "Tell us what you see while you have new eyes." When we are seeing a thing for the first time, our view is more objective. After we have looked at it repeatedly we begin to miss some things or assume some things. This happens with Scripture.

You are familiar with Matthew 18 as a chapter on forgiveness, and perhaps the prayer of agreement and binding and loosing, but the context of Jesus' teaching is about restoring fallen mankind to the childlike characteristics of innocence, spontaneity, fearlessness, and trust. There was a time before the child had fear, suspicion, prejudice and judgmentalism trained into her. The chapter is really about the Father's plan and purpose to restore us to *shalom* (wholeness). Let's look at it with new eyes.

> *At that time the disciples came to Jesus, saying, "Who then is greatest in the kingdom of heaven?" Then Jesus called a little child to Him, set him in the midst of them and said, "Assuredly, I say to you, unless you are converted* [strephō—turn back] *and become as little children, you will by no means enter the kingdom of heaven. Therefore, whoever humbles himself as this little child is the greatest in the kingdom of heaven. Whoever receives one little child like this in My name receives Me.*
>
> Matthew 18:1-5

Note this important part:

*Whoever causes one of these little ones who believe in Me to sin,
it would be better for him if a millstone were hung around his neck,
and he were drowned in the depth of the sea.*

Matthew 18:6

What Your Child Already Has That You Need

What are the characteristics of a child? Everyone knows that children are born with innocence, a sense of dependence, and an insatiable thirst for learning. The bumps and bruises of life will mar the innocence, but most of the other qualities have to be trained out of a child. There is something incredibly dynamic about the natural development of a child that may point to something of God's desire for us in coming into the Kingdom of God. Perhaps Jesus is saying more than we have assumed.

Can we learn anything about childlikeness by understanding a little one's early development? Without getting lost in the scientific weeds, it might help to know that at birth an infant's brain is 25 percent of the baby's total weight. Research has shown that most of the brain's actual physical growth occurs during the first two years of life, when powerful neural connections are made in response to the child's environment. At birth, there are roughly 100 billion neurons already developed in a child's brain. Those neurons are tentative connections, which become hardwired through the child's experiences. I want to repeat this because it is such a huge key to its spiritual parallel in the *Abba Formation*: the neurons that start as billions of tentative connections get "hardwired" (become permanent highways for neuro-communication) *through the child's experiences*. These connections will be responsible for all of a child's major intellectual and emotional functioning, including vision, language, emotions, and movements. During this highly accelerated rate of growth, these 100 billion neurons will each be responsible to make 15,000 connections until the process maxes-out by the age of ten or so, after which few will be produced for the rest of the child's life. Child development experts assert that by the age of three, 85 percent of all the child's fundamental structures of knowledge are formed. By the age of ten, the child will have twice as many neuro-connections as an adult.

Paul makes a connection between real spiritual transformation and a lived-out experience. It is important to note that the genetic foundations of the infant, combined with its environment (early relational experiences) will be the primary determining factors in the development of the child. Early experiences have definitive impact upon the architecture of the brain and the nature and extent of adult capacities. In other words, early childhood events and interactions don't just create a context, they directly affect the brains development.

In case you just checked out or got lost in the scientific details, let me make a connection for you. We saw in the previous chapter that Paul came to Corinth having realized that head knowledge (eloquent words of men's wisdom and philosophies) didn't yield supernatural fruit. He came to Corinth ready to combine his preaching and teaching with demonstrations of the Spirit's power (1 Cor. 1:4). In other words, Paul makes a connection between real spiritual transformation and a lived-out experience. Just hold that thought as we develop the connection further.

Characteristics of a Child

Jesus called a child to come stand in front of Him—something of an object lesson for His teaching. We have interpreted Jesus' intention as though He is saying, "Unless you become humble like this child (and all children) you can't access the realm of God" (Matt. 18:4). But this would infer that there is something we need to work on, try harder, or perfect. Jesus is not pointing to a special quality this child had worked to develop, but rather to the absence of sophistication, experiences, and hard knocks. Vincent's Greek Word Studies explains that "this is not about the child humbling himself, but what the child is by nature."[13]

Children are innocent, fearless, dependent, not self-conscious, transparent, dreamers, imaginative, energetic, learners, impartial, non-prejudiced, and relational—just to name a few. For the sake of focus, let's consider just four of these characteristics.

1. Children are Fearless (until taught to be fearful)

The humility of little children has much to do with their innocence in the sense that they don't fear. They do not know to be afraid because they are unaware of most of the world beyond a few feet away. These little ones have not experienced the "darker side" of a brutal world and learned to be fearful. In a very unsettling sense for a parent, a little child is fearless. Children are trained to be fearful when adults show them the bad things that could happen. What is Jesus saying to us about fearlessness?

2. Children are Carefree and Spontaneous

Children are also generally gregarious. They aren't normally self-conscious because they haven't spent time in front of the mirror. They squeal, cry, sing, blabber, cry some more. They are experimenting with their voices. In this way they are great relational connectors! A toddler can be sitting in the baby-seat of a grocery basket while mom is loading the groceries onto the checkout counter. The little one does not know that anyone would not like her. She is the center of the world. She is waving at everyone, saying "hi," and suddenly you find yourself telling the mother how cute the baby is, and you have made a new friend because of the freedom and spontaneity of this child.

On the other hand, it is also easy to spot a child who has been trained to fear. That child sees a new face suspiciously, doesn't talk, hides behind mom or dad when a stranger approaches, and so on. (Please don't get sidetracked on the many other reasons why this happens; it is a generalization to make a point).

Our niece, Nati, was so guileless as a little one that when she knew she had done something her parents probably wouldn't approve of, she would share it transparently and grin! It was as though there was no awareness that someone would ever not love her. She was so secure in her family's love that nothing was hidden. It didn't take long for that to get reprogrammed in her thinking (as is the case for all of us). As children grow older they get scolded for a transgressing behavior and realize some things might displease someone. Then they learn the feelings of rejection, the power of people-pleasing, and how to self-protect. Could Jesus be implying that life in the Kingdom is more about being carefree and spontaneous—a way of being the real you—rather than cunning and calculating?

3. Children are Naturally Trusting

A baby starts its journey as totally dependent upon her parents and has no concept of lack of trust. A little one cannot conceive that she should be

Could it be that sonship has to do with hearing what the Father is saying, and obeying instead of analyzing? worrying about where the next meal is coming from. That little one may very well be hungry for lack of care, but doesn't know anything beyond "I'm hungry." It is only when promises are made and broken, or when expectations go unfulfilled that these little ones become fearful, suspicious and mistrusting.

On a merely human level, even the best of parents may create (accidentally or intentionally) some expectation in a child that goes unfulfilled. A parent may unwisely use a "we'll stop at Chick-fil-A" as a way to pacify a child, then not build enough time into the busy schedule of errands to make the stop. The child learns mistrust.

Isn't it interesting that God places such an emphasis on His own faithfulness and trustworthiness so that we will believe Him when He makes a promise? He declares:

> *Indeed I have spoken it;*
> *I will also bring it to pass.*
> *I have purposed it;*
> *I will also do it.*

Isaiah 46:11

Could our spiritual transformation be about a restoration of total trust in a Father who knows what we have need of before we ask? Could it be that sonship has to do with hearing what the Father is saying, and obeying instead of analyzing?

4. Children are Naturally Creative

We can easily lose sight of the natural creativity in children when they are surrounded with so many toys, tools and technology that the creativity has been done for them. If you travel to developing countries where many children grow up in poverty, you will see creativity abounding. The boys play "baseball" with a stick for a bat and yarn, trash (or anything they can roll up) for a ball. I've seen young people play a tin can attached to a flat board with wires strung the length of the board as a makeshift guitar. Who hasn't seen a child line up some dolls to preach or teach to them?

The same is true for spiritual creativity. Believers should be writing the most powerful songs in the world, creating the most awe-inspiring sounds, and patenting the greatest inventions. With the Creator Spirit living within us—the same Spirit who hovered over the face of the deep in the beginning just waiting for a Word to be spoken—should the Church not be leading the world on tour into the majesty of God? Certainly, Peter quoted Joel's prophecy to say this very thing.

Creativity is restored to those who are restored to childlikeness by the Spirit of Adoption.

> *And it shall come to pass in the last days, says God,*
> *That I will pour out of My Spirit on all flesh;*
> *Your sons and your daughters shall prophesy,*
> *Your young men shall see visions,*
> *Your old men shall dream dreams.*
>
> Acts 2:17

Creativity is restored to those who are restored to childlikeness by the Spirit of Adoption.

The primary role of the Holy Spirit is to convince and convict us of a restored Sonship—to make us into innocent, fearless, spontaneous, trusting children again. He does this by releasing the *Abba Cry* in our hearts (Rom. 8:17; Gal. 4:1, 2). Jesus said the Holy Spirit will convict us of our righteousness (John 16:8); that is, bring us to the conviction again that we are the sons of God, and that God is a good Father.

How We Lose Our Childlikeness

Jesus brings a child to stand in front of the crowd and says:

> *Assuredly, I say to you, unless you are converted* [return to]
> *and become as little children, you will by no means enter*
> *the kingdom of heaven.*
>
> Matthew 18:3

Then He begins to talk about how we offend each other, how we cause one another to sin. He says that even if a member of our body offends us, we should get rid of it. He is painting a picture of how transient this life is, but how eternal the wounds we inflict can be. The foot will be restored with the resurrected body and the hand will be restored with the resurrected body, but the damage we do to one another can have eternal impact. Jesus even says, in effect, that it's not the cause-and-effect reality of the broken world that is offensive to God, but the broken relationships therein. God is relational by nature and wants our relationships to be whole. This is why Jesus then says:

> *Again I say to you that if two of you agree on earth*
> *concerning anything that they ask, it will be done for them*
> *by My Father in heaven.*
> Matthew 18:19

He loves it when His sons and daughters live in a shared life of agreement.

What every parent sees when he sees that child standing in front of Jesus is a life of potential and unfulfilled prophetic promise. God has hardwired every person with certain gifts and talents that, when developed, will help lead them to their destiny. Those dreams and aptitudes, however, get crushed when siblings berate them, stressed-out parents exasperate them, classmates bully them, and the scar tissue around their young hearts chokes out the carefree personality and the dreams. We get pressed into the mold of public opinion, conformity, and a contagious disease called the status quo.

Where Did The "Genius" Go?

What happens between that early developmental time when children are fearless and full of dreams and the day when being average seems like a foregone conclusion? Howard Gardner, in his Harvard study called Project Zero, sought to develop intelligence tests for infants and toddlers. In the process he discovered something remarkable. The researchers found that almost all infants and toddlers up to age four tested at a genius level in the areas of his "multiple frames of intelligence" (spatial, kinesthetic, musical, interpersonal, mathematical, intrapersonal, and linguistic). By the age of ten, however, the percentage of children who tested at the genius level had dropped to 10 percent, and those over twenty years old had dropped to only two percent.[14]

"It didn't go anywhere; it's just been covered over by the voice of judgment."

Where did the genius go? What caused the plunge as the years went by? Michael Ray, in his follow-up research to Gardner's work says, "It didn't go anywhere; it's just been covered over by the voice of judgment."[15] This voice of judgment Ray speaks of is the fear, judgment, and ridicule that gets played over and over as a script in the mind, suffocating the genius that resides in the person. "That's a stupid idea." "You'll never amount to anything." "Why can't you be like your brother?" "When will you snap out of it?" or even something as innocent-sounding as "Don't quit your day job."

Remember, it's not just the genetics we are born with that affect our life, but the environment, relational exchanges, and nurturing (or lack thereof). According to scientists and sociologists, early experiences have definitive impact upon the architecture of the brain and the nature and extent of our adult capacities. Clearly, I am using childhood developmental science the same way Jesus did, as a metaphor of spiritual things. Please make the spiritual connections as we go.

Very Real Impacts of Abuse

Make your own spiritual applications when we talk about childhood traumas that damage the natural genius in children. Adverse Childhood Experiences (ACE) is terminology now used in a movement to measure the psychological and physiological effects in adults related to their childhood traumas.[16] The researchers surveyed 17,500 over the past twenty years, observing physical, emotional or sexual abuse, physical or emotional neglect, parental mental illness, substance dependence, incarceration, parental separation or divorce, or domestic violence. Then the research correlated to what degree those adverse childhood experiences impacted adult or lifelong health. Two striking discoveries came to the surface.

First, ACEs are incredibly common. 67 percent of the population had at least one or two childhood traumas (ACE), and 12.6 percent had four or more areas of trauma. Secondly, they observed a "dose-response" relationship between ACEs and health outcomes.[17] The higher one's ACE childhood trauma score, the worse one's adult health outcomes.

Satan uses traumatic experiences in our childhood as entry points to "steal, kill, and destroy" (John 10:10).

Here are some hard sociological facts that should inform our spiritual understanding. Satan uses traumatic experiences in our childhood as entry points to "steal, kill, and destroy" (John 10:10). Those adults who experienced four or more childhood trauma areas were two and a half times more likely to have chronic pulmonary disease (COPD). They are also two and a half times more likely to contract hepatitis, four and a half times more victimized by depression, and twelve times more likely to be suicidal. The hard data also revealed that those with seven or more ACEs had three times the incidents of lung cancer, and three and a half times the incidents of heart disease (the number 1 killer in the U.S.).[18] Dr. Nadine Harris says, "We now understand better than we ever have before how the exposure to early childhood adversity affects the brain and bodies of children."[19]

This is not even factoring in the biggest piece of the equation—the human heart! Imagine the havoc the enemy wreaks on humanity through the wounds and pains inflicted upon the spirit and the soul! Could this be why Jesus pronounces a dire warning on those who hinder people from living in childlikeness?

Let me restate that I am not primarily referring to natural childhood, though the similarities of cause and effect are now obvious by hard data. I am primarily pointing to the reality of the spiritual warfare that produces the orphan lie—how the enemy comes to bind up the soul of every man and woman with wounding words. The words and wounds are the Trojan horse that Satan uses to get you to believe lies about who God is and who we are.

How Do We Offend (*Skandalizō*) One of These Little Ones?

The words and wounds are the Trojan horse that Satan uses to get you to believe lies about who God is and who we are.

- We offend spiritual children by **retraining them from fearlessness to fearfulness** with questions such as, "What will people think of you if you do that?"
- We offend them by **retraining them from other-centered to self-centered, from carefree to self-focused.** How much of our preaching today is self-centered at the core and sets us up for offense?

- We offend them by **scarring their innocence with guilt and shame**.
- We offend them by **telling others in subtle ways that unless they behave a certain way, we can't accept them**. How much of our Christian experience is more conformity to a norm than experimenting in New Life?
- We offend them by **correcting them outside the safe environment of unconditional love** (Gal. 6:1-5).
- We offend them by **scoffing at their creativity, suggesting that there is only one right way to be and to do**. Our churches should be safe places where creativity is fostered and celebrated.
- We offend them by **putting burdens on them that we exempt ourselves from**. That is Pharisaism; ministry that values *what we do* and *how we do* it rather than *who we are*, is offensive to childlikeness.

As you can see, this is not just about toddlers. This is about how we treat each other. This is a dire warning that our new kingdom-reality is childlikeness and the thing Satan wants to do is scar and mar the new creation. This is of paramount importance to Jesus. When He stands this child in front of Him, He says, "It is better for you to have a millstone hung around your neck and be thrown into the sea than to be party to offending the childlikeness in a little one." Is it any wonder the New Testament Scriptures are so strong on affirming and commending one another rather than slandering, gossiping and backbiting?

Every time we insult someone, reject someone, hurt someone, or discount someone (perhaps even accidentally by not understanding how God made them in unique ways different from ourselves), we play a role in robbing them of the innocence, freedom and fearlessness of childlikeness. Our words put a wound on the soul of a brother or sister, which becomes an entry point for Satan to steal their fearlessness, trust and faith. The devastating thing about this in kingdom terms is that wounds produce isolation and mistrust. Blame and shame drive us further from one another (the opposite of God's kingdom design), but the Holy Spirit comes to restore childlike words in our hearts and the relationships that make us whole.

Every time we insult someone, reject someone, hurt someone, or discount someone, we play a role in robbing them of the innocence, freedom and fearlessness of childlikeness.

Telling the Stories

A successful businessman, loving husband, and father of four beautiful children wrote to me one day after hearing me speak on the contrast between the orphan spirit and the spirit of sonship. He said:

> I struggle a great deal with insecurity and as you were talking last night it seemed so obvious that I display the symptoms of someone with an orphan spirit. In addition, it's clear that I don't know who I am.
>
> This is a difficult topic for me because I've sat through the spiritual freedom classes that deal with this stuff and I've read books about it. I could probably recite to you a list of 25 things the Bible says about my identity, but I just struggle to believe that it's true about me. I feel disqualified. I'm afraid that I'll go through the rest of my life feeling this way, unsure of my standing before God.
>
> On top of that I have a great deal of difficulty sorting out the emphasis in Scripture on obedience and the truth that understanding who I am in Christ is more important. It's not that I don't want to believe it. I just don't understand.

This is not an unusual case. In fact, I use it because it is so typical. We have preached to the Church that if we behave in certain ways God will be pleased, and we will be fulfilled and happy. So, we do them. We jump through the hoops, read the Bible, pray every day, and expect to grow, grow, grow. What is missing, however, is not an external process of performance but an internal engine of change that reconnects us to who we are in a childlike state.

What if it is really true that "if any man be in Christ, he is a new creation; old things have passed away and all things have become new" (2 Cor. 5:17)? What if the issue is not "trying to be a better Christian" or "struggling to believe it"? What if we are trying to apply all of the operating principles and protocols of the Tree of the Knowledge of Good and Evil rather than climbing down from that performance tree and learning to abide in the Tree of Life? What if there is a way to get your childhood genius back, but it is not by understanding or comprehending with your mind? Would you be open to it?

How to Get Your Genius Back

In the previous chapter we explored several verses of 1 Corinthians 2 to show how the indwelling Holy Spirit, who dwells both within us and within the Trinity simultaneously, searches the Father's heart (His purposes and plans for us) and then downloads those thoughts and plans into our spirits. In this chapter I have asserted that this *Abba Cry* points us to a blueprint the Lord has for us to childlikeness as a way of being. I have suggested that the enemy comes to destroy our childlikeness with traumatic experiences, slanderous words, and criticisms that cause us to lose trust, spontaneity, fearlessness, and creativity. I have suggested that our "genius" didn't go anywhere, but it is still within, waiting to be restored and released again. Let's dig just a bit deeper on this idea.

The last two verses of 1 Corinthians 2 give us the biblical definition for "genius" as God has defined it. Paul says:

> *But he who is spiritual judges all things, yet he himself is rightly judged by no one.*
>
> 1 Corinthians 2:15

J.B. Philips paraphrase says:

> *The man of the Spirit has an insight into the meaning of everything, though he is not understood by the man of the world.*
>
> 1 Corinthians 2:15

The man of the Spirit is the "spiritual man," which is Paul's focus in this passage. It is the one who is taught by the Spirit (v. 14), receiving in his spirit what the Holy Spirit is downloading—those things freely given to us by the Father (vv. 10, 12).

Think about this with me. What does "genius" mean to you? Someone so smart that we can't figure out how they know what they know or do what they do? Someone who can connect seemingly unrelated concepts or principles that, when connected, explode into a new concept, invention, or paradigm? Your dictionary will say something to the effect of, "an exceptional

The man of the Spirit has an insight into the meaning of everything, though he is not understood by the man of the world.

intellectual or creative power or other natural ability." Contrast that with what God says. God's definition of "genius" is having insight into everything, but not being understood by natural thinking. The man of the Spirit is so far ahead of the curve, that the smartest of the smart guys of this world can't keep up.

Genius on Display

Do you want to see genius in action? Watch Jesus spit on the dust of the ground, make some clay, put it on a blind man's eyes, and suddenly the blind man sees. Notice Elisha's solution for one of his pupils who has dropped an ax head to the bottom of the pond:

> *So the man of God said, "Where did it fall?" And he showed him*
> *the place. So he cut off a stick, and threw it in there; and he made*
> *the iron float. Therefore he said, "Pick it up for yourself."*
> *So he reached out his hand and took it.*
>
> 2 Kings 6:6

Find the brightest physicists on the planet and ask them how that works!

Go with Moses into Pharaoh's palace and watch him throw down a rod which turns into a large snake, turns water into blood, and parts the Red Sea. The same wooden stick breaks a rock open and water starts pouring out. The list is long.

You see, your genius is, and always has been, centered in the Holy Spirit in your spirit. None of that is possible without God, but all things are possible with God (Mark 10:27). You will never find that kind of genius at work where the Holy Spirit is not working. Paul clearly says the man who learns to partner with the Holy Spirit will have insights into everything, but no one void of the Spirit will be able to figure out how he does what he does. He will almost look like superman, or better yet, like Adam before he sinned and lost his relationship with God. By the way, have you ever wondered how Adam gardened the entire territory between the Tigris and Euphrates rivers before he sinned? It would have looked totally supernatural from our natural point of view.

The objective of the Holy Spirit is to restore you and me to our potential and purpose in God!

In a profound way, this points to the objective of the Holy Spirit is to restore you and me to our potential and purpose in God! My pastor used to say, "If you hang out with the Holy Spirit, He will make you look smart." Perhaps this is what the Apostle John means when he says:

> *But the anointing which you have received from Him abides in you, and you do not need that anyone teach you; but as the same anointing teaches you concerning all things, and is true, and is not a lie, and just as it has taught you, you will abide in Him.*
>
> 1 John 2:27

The final verse of 1 Corinthians 2 has generally been grossly misunderstood, but it shows us how this inner genius works. Again, Paul quotes from the Old Testament (Isa. 40:13) to highlight the contrast between the old and new:

> *For who has known the mind of the Lord that we may instruct Him? But we have the mind of Christ.*
>
> 1 Corinthians 2:16

Jesus told His disciples, "Don't try to do this without first being filled with the Spirit" (Luke 24:49; Acts 1:4), but "once you receive the Spirit, you will be doing the same things you've seen Me do" (John 14:12).

How is that possible? Paul's answer is that we now have the mind of Christ! Of course, the context insists that we understand that the mind of Christ is not imparted to our minds (our brains), which is the common assumption, but in our spirits by the indwelling Holy Spirit! Every other sentence in this passage is talking about man's spirit, not his natural mind.

Paul is saying the same thing Jesus said but in different terminology. Jesus is imparting to us everything He has received from the Father by the indwelling Holy Spirit. The "mind of Christ" are the thoughts, will, plan, and purpose of God shared with us as His sons and daughters. We are no longer servants, but friends, because He tells us what He is doing (John 15:15).

You have the Genius of the universe, the Holy Spirit, living inside of you. You have the One who hovered over the darkness, took the words from God, "Let there be light," and created light,

You have the Genius of the universe, the Holy Spirit, living inside of you.

matter, the 100 billion galaxies, and every living thing. You have the Holy Spirit, who knows how everything in this universe works, because it is His handiwork. He is sharing with you what you need to know about the Father's plans and purposes for you, and "no good thing will He withhold from those who walk uprightly" (Ps. 84:11)!

Is your mind telling you, "Well, that certainly doesn't seem true for me. There are a lot of things I don't know, problems that I don't have answers for, and I don't think I'm smart enough to figure it out"? That's good. We need to understand that we will never have all the answers in our minds. But we also need to understand that:

> *We have an unction from the Holy One that abides within us and we know all things. We have an unction from the Holy One* [in our spirits], *and our dependence is not upon the limitations of natural understanding.*
> 1 John 2:20, 27 (my paraphrase)

Keep reading to discover how to access what is in your spirit.

What Have We Said?

Jesus brought a child in front of Him and told us that we must return to that kind of childlikeness to experience the realm of God here and now.

We explored some characteristics of childlikeness that the Holy Spirit restores to sons and daughters.

Some sociological and neurological studies show that genius is built into humanity.

We listed ways in which we offend others and put a gag of self-consciousness on their childlikeness.

The Bible definition of genius as found in 1 Corinthians 2:15-16.

PRAYER

Father, thank You for sending Your Spirit to restore my childlikeness. Sometimes I feel like "all work and no play makes Johnny a dull boy." Would You restore my joy again? Come, Holy Spirit, and anoint me (and all my family) with the oil of gladness. Restore my creativity, my fearlessness, and even a child-like spontaneity again. I roll my cares upon You. I choose to rejoice in Your goodness and unfailing love! Lord, I want to be that child standing in front of You, not worried about the cares of this world but carefree in what You have planned and how You are bringing to pass everything You have said in my life. Lord Jesus, I ask You to come in and heal those areas where slander, criticism, and judgments have put a gag on the genius of the Spirit in me. I forgive them. Forgive me wherever or whenever I might have been used by the enemy to damage the childlikeness in someone else. Yes, I'm going to say it. Holy Spirit, please restore the genius that was designed in me from the beginning. Fill me, Lord, with Your Spirit and grant dreams and visions that are beyond my natural capacities as I walk in Your Spirit. I trust You. You watch over every promise to fulfill it. Now, is there something You would like to say to me right now? I'm listening. Selah.

GROUP DISCUSSION

1. When Jesus brought the child to stand as a picture of the way to experience the Kingdom, what was He saying?

2. List some characteristics of childlikeness that we can expect the Holy Spirit to restore in us, and discuss why these might be important for our restoration.

3. Review the list of some of the ways we offend one-another and damage the childlikeness. Do any of them speak to your own history?

4. What is the Bible definition of genius as revealed in 1 Corinthians 2:15-16, and what kind of questions does that raise in you?

Four

The Gardener of the Soul

Mack looking at the garden said, "Even though there's still a lot of work to be done, I feel strangely at home and comfortable here."
"And well you should, Mackenzie," Sarayu (Holy Spirit) said, "because this garden is your soul."

– Wm. Paul Young

The Holy Spirit is the active ingredient for our transformation, giving us utterance, forming the words in our spirits, and drawing us into partnership in the transformation process. Using a different metaphor, our transformation is like a masterful gardener's patient work—uprooting emotional and spiritual weeds that choke the life out of people and planting the garden of God in every willing participant.[20]

In William Paul Young's masterful fiction, *The Shack*, a father named Mack has spiraled into a hopeless depression after the abduction and murder of his daughter. He is led back to the deep woods cabin where the little one was murdered to face his despair or possibly even find the murderer. He encounters the Trinity there in ways that demolish all his defaults about what God is like. In Young's portrayal, the Holy Spirit is wearing overalls and working in a garden. Mack remarks at how chaotic the garden looks, not aware that it is actually his own soul.[21]

As the Holy Spirit answers his suspicious inquiries, she (portrayed as a small Asian woman in the dream) has him dig a hole in the garden, which becomes significant at the end of the story. Mack is oblivious to the fact that the Holy Spirit has been diligently tending to the garden of his heart, cleaning out the weeds of woundedness and the thorns of unforgiveness, preparing the soil for new planting long before he had questions. At the end of the story, an amazing floral display of diverse shapes and brilliant colors have grown in this garden of Mack's soul—almost defying imagination in their beauty— depicting the healing that has been transpiring in Mack's heart.

The Holy Spirit is continuing the ministry of Jesus to heal the brokenhearted and set the captives free. He is uprooting the lies you have believed about God and, therefore, about yourself. In place of those weeds, beautiful creations for only you are planted. The gardening is just another way of saying what Jesus said to His disciples, "I am converting you back to the way you were as a child—in innocence, transparency, connectedness, security, potential and promise." Just how did Jesus say this would happen?

Jesus stood up in the synagogue on the Sabbath and opened the scroll to read. He read from the prophecy of Isaiah 61:

> *The Spirit of the Lord is upon me,*
> *because He has anointed me*
> *to proclaim good news to the poor.*
> *He has sent me to proclaim liberty to the captives*
> *and recovering of sight to the blind,*
> *to set at liberty those who are oppressed*
> *to proclaim the acceptable year of the Lord's favor.*
> Luke 4:18-19 (ESV)

The Holy Spirit is at work within you. It is the Spirit of the Lord that rests upon and within you.

Not Just Trimming the Hedges

We have grossly underestimated our good Father's power and His intentions in sending His Son. We have bought into a notion of a small God who is too anemic to be in the presence of sin, as if sin was more powerful than God. We have wrongly interpreted the Old Testament to say that God is a germaphobe who can neither stand in the presence of sin, nor be interested in being close to us as sinners—thus the seemingly endless rules laid upon His children to "touch no unclean thing." Whether consciously or subconsciously, we have thought God prohibits the eating of certain "unclean" foods or the exposure to lepers, prostitutes, and sinners for the sake of His perfectionism rather than our protection. We have thought this shrunken God is happy to just trim our rotten hedges to keep us looking good, rather than get dirty in the garden of our souls.

Jesus, however, came to correct our mistaken notions of God. He didn't avoid the contagious leper. He boldly walked up to the leper, put His hands upon him and healed him. They had never seen this before. This is the revelation of not only the all-powerful God, but also the all-loving "witness" God who never intended or desired to allow any distance between man and Himself. Jesus shocked the religious folks by regularly dining and conversing with sinners, tax collectors, prostitutes, Samaritans, and even the religious! He was so secure in His identity of strength in love that He was comfortable with and welcoming of everyone. We have underestimated God because we have projected a God in our own image (though super-sized to mythological proportions).

In the same way, we have grossly underestimated God by our notions of salvation. For many Christians, the Gospel is not much more than a ticket to Heaven—an escape from a polluted world that is just too rotten, too dirty, too far gone for redemption. We have not understood that salvation includes the empowering of the believer, by the indwelling Spirit, to have mastery over sin. The Christian game is to get sinners to say a prayer, get born again, then tie a knot on the end of the rope and hang on until you die or Jesus comes. We have not understood the power of the cross nor its immediate impacts upon our spirit, soul and body. We have not grasped Paul's declaration:

Reckon yourselves to be dead indeed to sin, but alive to God in Christ Jesus our Lord. Therefore do not let sin reign in your mortal body, that you should obey it in its lust ....
For sin shall not have dominion over you.
Romans 6:11-14

Restoration at The Genetic Level

Though we know that our bodies will not experience full redemption until corruption puts on incorruption at Jesus' return (1 Cor. 15:52-57), we should know that the same Spirit that raised Christ from the dead—the Holy Spirit—dwells within us. If this is so, is there any possibility that God-in-us would not have a real and powerful effect on every part of our being, including health and wholeness for our bodies?

Interestingly, a fairly new science has developed called Epigenetics. It is a study of how our genes are modified by various actors, especially nutrition

Could the Holy Spirit's work in me actually break generational patterns of abuse and bondage in my family?

and environment. Up until the last twenty years or so it was assumed that our DNA was fixed and unalterable. However, research on the impacts of the Netherlands Famine just after World War II has revealed that several environmental factors have had long-term effects upon those born during the famine. This implies that the activities and environment of one generation can impact subsequent generations, and the new research raises the question of whether this could even extend to the cellular level. This prospect of biological alterations at a cellular level opens a new horizon of possibility. Richard Francis says, "Epigenetic changes occur in response to our environment, the foods we eat, the pollutants to which we are exposed, even our social interactions."[22] This includes repeated behaviors (habits) that cause some genes to be turned on or off, which can potentially leave the next generation more susceptible to certain conditions or free from them.

For example, are there biological impacts upon an alcoholic that cause his children and grandchildren to be more susceptible to alcoholism? Certainly, the psychological impacts of alcoholism have been traced to the subsequent generations.[23] Physiological research suggests that the child of an alcoholic may possess a higher tolerance for alcohol, making him more likely to drink excessively without realizing the onset of alcoholism, thus repeating the cycle. What about chronic worriers, those addicted to pornography, or to certain foods?

Epigenetics research also shows some early indications of transgenerational effects in human beings, some direct and some indirect. "One of these is called genomic imprinting in which the original epigenetic mark in the parent is reproduced with great fidelity in the offspring."[24] What could this mean? That a person's continued actions or responses could actually reshape the genetic make-up of a person by turning some genes on or off.

If this is the case, the question must be asked whether spiritual redemption can have similar positive effects at physiological levels. That is, am I bound inextricably to my habits, and do I naturally pass those weaknesses down to my children, or is real transformation possible? Could the Holy Spirit's indwelling work impact how I break free and maintain that freedom from habits of the past? What if I could turn off a gene that makes me susceptible to overeating, for example? Not only that, but could the Holy Spirit's work in me actually break generational patterns of abuse and bondage in my family? This is important. Remember the Bible speaks of the sins of our fathers being passed down to the third and fourth generations.

By breaking the cycles of sin in my own life, I set up the generations after me for victory.

What does this mean? It may only point to the reality that the more we consistently obey the indwelling impulses of the Spirit (Rom. 8:13) the stronger our mental (neurological) connections become, and the more our very physiology gets "renewed" to become "instruments of righteousness" rather than weakened tools of sin. In other words, the Holy Spirit within us, aided by our active obedience in partnership to His voice, can effect such a transformation in us that the temptations—the psychological and physiological pull that once held such a powerful grip—can be starved out by lack of environment and repetition. Better yet, by breaking the cycles of sin in my own life, I set up the generations after me for victory.

Do you know what is more freeing than having the willpower to conquer a temptation? Not having the temptation in the first place! I am not suggesting that you or I can ever come to a place in this lifetime where we have no temptations. I am saying that if you make the Holy Spirit your best friend, what held you in the past doesn't have the right or power to hold you in the future. I am saying that the addictions and struggles of your past are not your identity, only your history.

Some Questions

What are we being set free from, and how does it happen? Isn't it really just about going to church regularly, acting nicer than the folks who don't go to church, and giving it your best shot? Is it about not making too much of a mess so you can get into heaven? Is there any expectation that God is working on an outrageously lavish garden in your soul that makes the whole of your existence beautiful? What are we being set free from, and is there any chance that we keep ourselves so busy that we don't know about the garden of our souls? Do you have any idea what

One thing we know: we are being set free from the lingering effects of Hell's attacks on our identity as sons and daughters of God.

It has been said that "the truth will set you free, but first it will make you miserable." the Holy Spirit is uprooting from your garden? Any idea as to what the Holy Spirit is planting in your garden?

One thing we know: we are being set free from the lingering effects of Hell's attacks on our identity as sons and daughters of God. Think of the worst images of war-torn cities you have ever seen, whether Aleppo, Syria, Mosul, Iraq, or Marinka, Ukraine. The sight of hundreds of empty, burned-out, shelled-out buildings are a fitting metaphor for the condition of many men's souls. However, what would be hopeless to man is simply the labor of love for the Triune God who overflows healing and wholeness as a way of being. Your heart is His prize, your soul His project. Hear again the mighty declaration of the Father, on the lips of Jesus, at His first synagogue message:

> *The Spirit of the Lord is upon me, anointing me to preach ... release ... give ... bind up ... and comfort ....*
>
> Luke 4:18-19

Jesus wasn't just preaching as we think of preaching today. Jesus was reasserting the declaration of war from Father's lips, first uttered in Genesis 3:15, that Satan's head would be crushed and God would fulfill the decree by being more than doing. Love always wins.

Jesus did not come dispensing information to the clamoring crowds who needed a sandwich and the latest rabbinical nuance. He came to transform people one by one by revealing who the Father really is, and Himself as *Abba's* Son. What He knew, and we should be learning, is that no amount of information will transform us. Jesus submitted to the Father in everything, including baptism at the hands of John. When He came up out of the water, the heavens opened, and the Father spoke His pleasure over the Son while filling Him with the Spirit without measure.

This idea of submitting to God by limiting ourselves and our rights is to participate in the difficult and sobering gardening work of the Spirit who will make a mess in our souls while beautifying them. It has been said that "the truth will set you free, but first it will make you miserable." We don't like to hear it, and it's one reason many of us avoid quiet moments, contemplative silence, and listening rather than talking. None of us, however, would dare assume that there is nothing in the garden of our souls that doesn't need the powerful loving hands of the Master Gardener.

What does this look like in practical ways? First, the Spirit may challenge your "rights" as Sarayu challenged Mack saying, "Rights are where survivors go so they won't have to work out relationships."[25] Don't ever think that the Holy Spirit, who walked with Jesus to the cross and beyond, is afraid to get a little dirty. I suspect the day will come, when we see Jesus face to face, that we will see nail prints in His hands. Then He will introduce us to the Holy Spirit, and we will see lots of dirt on His/Her hands as well (we understand that God is spirit and does not have a gender, except for the male humanity of Jesus).

Examining the Gardener's Work

Let's examine the Gardener's work more closely, and as we do, why not ask Him to cultivate some new ground in you? Let a whisper come upon your lips as you read, *"Do more of that, Lord. Do more of that in me."* Since the work of the soul is a partnership, perhaps then you will hear the Holy Spirit say what Sarayu said to Mack, *"Grab that shovel and dig up that area right there."* This partnership is seen by the *"Abba Cry"*—the Holy Spirit gives utterance (forms the words) but our spirits do the speaking. I strongly believe that the Holy Spirit is patient to only work where we are willing to partner with Him. Here are some priorities in the Garden of the Soul:

1. The *Abba Cry* releases us from the slavery of wounded ways and thinking (Gal. 4:3-9).

The Spirit of God in you cries *"Abba,* Father" and effects a process of transformation from slave thinking and low living to sonship realities. Interestingly, the same root word Jesus used (*strephō*) when He brought the child to stand with Him (Matt. 18:2-5), Paul uses to ask the believers at Galatia, "How is it that you turn again (*epistrephō*) to the weak and beggarly elements, to which you desire again to be in bondage?" (Gal. 4:9). What does that slave thinking look like? This kind of thinking assumes a "might is right," "dog eat dog," "step on a few folks on your way to the top" kind of world that is all about survival and looking out for self. This "returning" can go both ways. We can return to childlike simplicity and trust, or we can return to the bondage of self-centered, top-down thinking.

We are called by Christ to "turn back" to childlikeness and cautioned by Paul not to "turn back" to the old ways of the world. The Holy Spirit forms the *Abba Cry* in us (through which our spirits are free and empowered to call God, "Daddy"), and this process is what recalibrates us to our position as sons.

What does this mean? It means we can resist the work of the Spirit, ignore the work of the Spirit, and even mock the work of the Spirit if we choose. God is very uncontrolling. The *Abba Cry* releases us from wounded ways of thinking and living as we learn to cooperate with Him—to feel the gentle nudge of the Spirit and whisper in response, "Speak Lord, I'm listening." "Do more work in me, oh, Holy Spirit."

More and more, I am learning that the Holy Spirit is interested in the condition of my heart. As trite as this sounds, the soil is the primary concern of a gardener. No matter how wonderful the flowers from the nursery may look, if they are planted in bad soil they will not thrive. How is your heart? Both slave-thinking and orphan- thinking will have a tendency to respond matter-of-factly, "Oh, I'm good. Everything's fine." However, learning to listen to the Father's voice is first about tending to your heart.

Do you have anyone in your life who can ask you how your heart is? If not, perhaps a good place to start is to ask the Lord to bring someone into your life who would care enough about you to ask the question and listen until there is a substantive answer. The Holy Spirit is the Great Networker. He knows how to bring people to you.

2. The Spirit's cry convinces us of our sonship (Rom. 8:14-16).

This is the primary and ongoing work of the Spirit in the believer, restoring us to full fellowship with our *Abba*. Paul tells the Roman believers that they (thus, we) did not receive a spirit of fear (certainly not from God), but we received the Holy Spirit, a spirit of adoption whereby we cry "*Abba,* Father." The Spirit himself testifies with our spirits that we are sons of God. As one paraphrase puts it:

God's Spirit touches our spirits and confirms who we really are.

God's Spirit touches our spirits and confirms who we really are.
We know who he is, and we know who we are: Father and children. And we know we are going to get what's coming to us
—an unbelievable inheritance!
Romans 8:16-17 (MSG)

Genesis says that humanity was made in the image and likeness of God, but image and likeness are two different things. The "image" of God cannot be removed from man. Those unchanging qualities such as free will, creativity, language, and vision/

I will not leave you orphans; I will come to you. John 14:18

imagination are God's image, replicated in humanity for the purposes of fellowship and dominion. The likeness, however, has been damaged. To be like God is to love, trust, give ourselves away in generosity, and to live in childlikeness. The likeness has been marred in man due to sin, and this is what the garden of our souls is about.

The Holy Spirit is actively at work conforming us into the likeness of Jesus. What is that likeness? Jesus is the perfect Son—fearless yet listening, innocent yet bold, submitted and relational. Gordon Fee, preeminent biblical scholar, says that the whole context of Romans 8 is that "by the Holy Spirit we are free from Torah observance, sin and death!" The rebellion has ended. The end result is "Like Father, like S/son."[26]

3. The *Abba Cry* activates a daily partnership with God that is beyond our imagination.

Many believers are simply trying to get to heaven, but Jesus said that we would be doing the same works He did because we have the same Spirit working in us (John 14:12). How can we have this assurance? Jesus himself tells us:

> *And I will pray the Father, and He will give you another Helper*
> *[paraclete just like me], that He may abide with you forever—the*
> *Spirit of truth … He dwells with you and will be in you.*
> John 14:16-17

Then He makes this astounding statement:

> *I will not leave you orphans; I will come to you.*
> John 14:18

Jesus is walking with you and in you right now by the indwelling Holy Spirit. This is the fulfillment and practical application of His promise:

Everything God does, He does in partnership by relationship.

I will never leave you nor forsake you.

Hebrews 13:5

Part of the byproduct of that indwelling presence is a God-inside-consciousness that shifts the way we see ourselves and the world around us. The Holy Spirit, through spiritual language, begins to make you constantly conscious that He is always in you, therefore you always have access not only to right or wrong, inside or outside, weak or strong, but the third option—another possibility that can't be seen without the Spirit. It is a God-consciousness that made a teenager named David trash-talk a nine-foot giant while running at him with a sling and stone. That God-inside mindedness propelled Jesus to call for twelve huge jars of water at a wedding when He hadn't done a single miracle yet. This God-consciousness caused Paul to lay handkerchiefs and cloths on his body knowing that the anointing from God would work special signs and miracles in those who were sick.

Everything God does He does in partnership, by relationship. He is a relational, three-and-one God. He doesn't do life as "the big Man upstairs" or "the monad in the sky." He does life relationally, thus partnership is His mode of operation. This means that if you have this idea that someday God is going to unilaterally "do something big," and it will just drop out of the sky, you might want to reconsider. He is looking for someone to partner with now—someone who will hear His voice and His heart now, and act. Notice in the verse above (Heb. 13:5) that God declares He will never leave us or forsake us. Then the writer of Hebrews instructs us in the practicality of the statement:

So we may boldly say:" The Lord is my helper;
I will not fear. What can man do to me?"

Hebrews 13:6

Do you see the partnership there? God has acted, so you and I will act with Him. The Holy Spirit is constantly working in us and calling us to act with God in the things that are on God's heart.

4. The *Abba Cry* restores fearlessness, spontaneity, and trust—renewing our childlike design.

We spent significant space in the previous chapter talking about our childlike design. Perhaps in the current trends of our day it should be clarified that this is not about standing in front of the mirror every morning and making bold declarations to convince yourself that something yet unseen is true. This is not about mind over matter. This is not about mustering the willpower to make something happen to prove we are somebody, and it is certainly not about obligating God to somehow come through for us because we stuck our neck out. This is about understanding that the Holy Spirit has taken up humanity's cause and is, moment by moment, forming words in your spirit that reshape your being into the likeness of the Son.

This will require some gardening. This will require the Holy Spirit getting into your mess, your woundedness, your stubbornness, your unforgiveness, your bad memories and nightmares. Yes; just as there are things we can do to cultivate relational equity and intimacy with our spouse, there are things we can do to participate in or to hinder this process of healing and freedom.

Partnership with the Holy Spirit

As a precursor to the next chapter I will offer some basic observations here. Western Christianity tends to skirt around this most fundamental issue. I want to say it plainly: we build ourselves up in the consciousness of who we really are by practicing the presence of God through worship, prayer, and in particular praying in the Holy Spirit. Jude says:

> *But you, beloved, building yourselves up on your most holy faith, praying in the Holy Spirit ....*
>
> Jude 1:20

Especially for those who like lists, let's answer the question, "How do I partner with the Holy Spirit in this *Abba Cry* process of childlikeness restoration?"

1. Humble yourself and come to Christ. He is Savior, and He is also the Baptizer in the Spirit (Mark 1:8).

Begin to give yourself away—your strengths, your talents, the things you love to do.

2. Invite Jesus to baptize you in the Holy Spirit (Luke 11:11-13). Say, "Lord, I want everything you have for me. Would You baptize me with Your Holy Spirit?"

3. Don't mistake an emotional experience for the overflowing other-centeredness of the Person.

4. Partner with the Holy Spirit in the spiritual language that releases the *Abba Cry* in you, rebuilding your childlike design (Rom. 8:16; 1 Cor. 14:2, 4).

5. Get ready to play, think, laugh, and dream like a kid again (Joel 2:28, Acts 2:17). Dreams and visions are restored wherever believers are filled with the Spirit.

6. Pray as the Spirit prompts you. The Holy Spirit will cultivate in you the child's perfect prayer: "*Abba*, I belong to You. Father in Heaven, I worship You." You will experience an enlargement in your soul that might be similar to trading in a drinking straw for a fire hose. This just means a greater capacity to experience God's presence in us.

7. Meditate (a spiritual process that causes a fire to burn in your spirit) on Scriptures that declare your sonship (Eph. 1:18-19).

8. Begin to give yourself away—your strengths, your talents, the things you love to do, are God's gifts through you for someone else (1 Pet. 4:10). To live in the fellowship of the Trinity is to learn to empty yourself continually. To empty yourself is to be full.

9. Spend time with others who are also cultivating their relationship with the Lord by the Holy Spirit—as iron sharpens iron (Heb. 10:24).[27]

Find others who are on the same journey of Spirit-fullness.

Here is a quick word about our inheritance as sons and the giving of gifts. One predictable mistake for new believers is to think that all these gifts that are flowing to us are just for our own benefit. If we don't understand that the Father is preparing a bride for His Son, we might just think all those wedding gifts are for us! Actually, He has placed us into a community of believers so that we can learn to get other-conscious rather than self-conscious. There is also a global transformation underway. God is filling the whole earth with the knowledge of His glory, which means the larger objective of your transformation and mine is not just to get us free so we can do what we wish. It is to see the whole earth filled with the goodness and glory of God!

Revisiting the "Joy Ride"

Before we move away from the idea of being restored to childlikeness, let's revisit the story of the red convertible mustang on the highway in Colorado that I share in *The Abba Factor*. If you read it in my earlier book, I ask you not to shortcut the process. As you read it, visualize the story. Ask the Father to talk to you about the steps you are taking in that "returning" (*strephō*) to childlikeness. What are you seeing now? What weeds, wounds, or lies is the Holy Spirit digging up in the garden of your soul?

Imagine a red convertible Mustang, top down, on a journey on the open road. This car is on the highway somewhere in Colorado in early summer, driving through a spacious landscape of lush, green pastureland. In the distance, to the right, are snow-peaked mountains, and on the left is a crystal-clear river running with that "clean Rocky Mountain" water. There are some cattle grazing in the open pastures (they must be the happiest cows in the world), and an occasional farmhouse in the distance. Do you see it?

As we zoom in on the five people in the red Mustang, everything seems so typical. Behind the wheel, driving with a certain serene calmness is the father of the family. He is clearly enjoying this experience of taking his family on this scenic adventure. There is a slight pleasant smile—the distilling of an unconscious delight—on the father's face as he seems to be taking his family back to a childhood home or a destination he has planned for them for some time. His left elbow rests on the driver's side door and his right arm stretched out straight ahead over the steering wheel, casually steering with ease. He's happy.

In the front passenger side seat is his wife. Her gaze is fixed on a smart phone in her hands as she studies her maps app to stay aware of the exact location of the vehicle and ensure her husband doesn't take a wrong turn.

Her hair is blowing in the wind as well, but it seems more of a bother—blocking her view of the small screen, covering her eyes again and again—so that she impatiently strokes her hair behind her ears to one side and then the other. She is quietly rehearsing how far they have traveled, the miles ahead, when they will need to make the next turn, and how far until the next gas station. She has not glanced upward to behold the surrounding beauty for some time now, but is a conscientious navigator.

In the smallish backseat (the Mustang wasn't mom's idea) are three children ranging in age from eight to fifteen. Sitting behind mom is the middle-aged of the three. She is troubled about the journey. She readily admits that she "doesn't travel well." She was traumatized by an accident a few years back, with some recurring dreams that have kept the memory fresh in her mind. She seems to be in pain, holding her face in her hands, bending over again and again, face down to her knees as she rocks back and forth hoping this journey ends soon with no terrible surprises! It seems the last thing on her mind is to look up and take in the beautiful scene surrounding them. Perhaps, one thinks, this is why the mother is so intent upon the navigation. The father is serenely, confidently driving, the mother is intently navigating, and this child seems at least troubled, almost traumatized.

In the back seat, on the left behind the father, is the oldest of the three—a son sporting large "noise reduction" headphones which are attached to a video game of some kind. He is oblivious to the surroundings and is only aware of the score he has been trying to beat for over a week now. He is detached from the real world, detached from the unforgettable scenery outside the car, detached from the family inside the car, detached from reality, except for an occasional hunger pain and sensation of thirst. He is also looking down, but slightly aware and annoyed that the youngest is being her usual animated self.

The youngest child is between the other two, but not sitting down. She is standing up—precariously—hands stretched out wide with squeals of glee. She is looking to the mountains, then to the river, then back to the pasturelands again. Over and over she shrieks, "Wow, Daddy, look at the mountains! Smell this fresh air! Have you ever seen anything like this before?" Your first thought, of course, is that standing up in the back seat of a fast-moving vehicle is dangerous. We as onlookers immediately glance back at the father expecting him to correct her and command her to "Sit!" Instead, we see the same easy smile across his face.

He is sharing in her joy; she is manifesting his. She **He is sharing in** is the only passenger who is actually appreciating the **her joy; she is** glory and beauty that surrounds—the purpose for **manifesting his.** which they have made this journey. He is somehow confident that she is safe in her ecstasy. With a brilliant grin, the playful daughter glances to the rearview mirror in front to see the reflection of her father's eyes—looking back through the same mirror at her. His experience allows him to casually "keep one eye" on the road and the other on her. They see each other and share the joy of creation as though they were one.

Does the father love this little one more than the others? Oh no. He loves his wife, of course, and all of them with all his heart, but he especially rejoices in the one who is rejoicing with him. His heart is full to know that this little one has no care, no fear, no thought of what could go wrong or when the next stop will be. She doesn't even fully realize that this, this moment, is what the trip is all about.

The Father, by the Spirit, through the Son, is lovingly restoring us, His children, to a childlikeness that sets us free from the bondage of fear. His Spirit is drawing us back to a place prior to being traumatized, wounded, disappointed, or discounted. He is setting us free from the need to either check out or perform. He has no fear that you will fall out of the car; that is only a fear that we project upon Him. He is bringing you to a place where you have nothing to hide, nothing to fear, nothing to prove, nothing to lose.

Do you find yourself in this prophetic scene? Do you identify with the mom who is so busy being responsible, calculating, analyzing, assessing, planning—so much so that you haven't looked up for a while to notice that God has surrounded you with awe and wonder? Look up and live! The Father has been down this road a million times. He knows how to get you there without missing a turn or running out of gas.

Do you identify with the traumatized daughter, so fearful of the journey? Maybe you dare not look due to previous traumas. You need to know that "the Father himself loves you" (John 16:27; 17:23) and will never leave you. Any whisper in your thoughts that He has already left you is a lie. Choose to believe that He is casually in control. Then you can enjoy this ride.

Do you identify with the video game boy who is detached from the father's good pleasure? Have you, for whatever reason, chosen to submerge yourself with another reality of your choosing? I would suggest that the first step is not to analyze the "why," but to acknowledge that you have been missing the scenery God has prepared for your life. Once you've seen it you can never "un-see" it.

Perhaps you would just want to say, "OK *Abba*, Daddy, if there is a world of wonder and adventure in You that I am missing, would You begin to draw me into it? Would You change the "want-tos" in me? I think You know how to get me to that place. I want to be the one standing in the back seat, wind blowing through my hair, overwhelmed at just how awesome You are.

This prophetic picture speaks to me of the Father's plan to restore us to childlikeness, making us ready for an eternal adventure that is too much for finite minds to comprehend. What I know is that it will take all of eternity for *Abba* to show off the glorious things He has prepared for those who love Him. Paul prays:

> *… that in the ages to come He might show the exceeding riches of His grace in His kindness toward us in Christ Jesus.*
>
> Ephesians 2:7

Ponder This:

The byproduct of maturing in oneness with *Abba* is restored childlikeness and with it an experienced tenderness and trusting innocence (in the Father). As we continue to submit ourselves to His tender partnership, our responses in any situation will be *Abba's* mission. Can a person say he is a Christian and receive *Abba's* love without that love producing a desire to express the same intimate love and compassion toward others? *Abba's* love does not handicap an individual. *Abba* does not just smother someone with physical attention. His love produces a warm, caring, and trusting environment through which a child feels unrestricted by fear or self-consciousness. By understanding who you are, developing spiritual gifts and talents and expressing them through healthy relationships, vocational and avocational adventure is now your earthly inheritance.

What Have We Said?

Our soul is like a garden that can have both beautiful flowers and weeds growing up together, and the Holy Spirit is the gardener, fully committed to lovingly cultivate our souls into a place of beauty.

We described four ways the Holy Spirit works in us via the *Abba Cry*.

Because God is a relational being, He does life as partnership. We listed numerous ways to partner with the Holy Spirit.

We explored "the Joy Ride" as a prophetic picture and asked which of the seats in the red convertible are we sitting in, that is, what is the condition of the soil of our souls?

PRAYER

Abba, I have no doubt that You love me totally and completely. Thank You, thank You, thank You. I also know that You love me too much to leave me in my brokenness and woundedness. I confess that I'm not that excited about having to deal with the mess that is in the garden of my soul, but I believe the Holy Spirit loves to get the weeds at their roots and clean out everything that has been sown as tares or weeds in my garden. I invite You, Holy Spirit, to come. I invite You to begin to uproot whatever needs to be uprooted. Speak and work gently in me, and I commit to partner with You in it. Whatever You tell me to do I will do. If I need to seek forgiveness, reach out to someone, or renounce something in my life, I am listening. I am counting on You to create and energize in me both the power and the desire to obey in every way. In Jesus' mighty name. Amen.

GROUP DISCUSSION

1. What was Jesus' understanding of what the Holy Spirit was doing in and through His ministry (Isa. 61; Luke 4:18-19)?

2. Which of the four works of the *Abba Cry* speaks to you the most?

3. Look at the list of ways to partner with the Holy Spirit. Which of those would you want to discuss further?

4. How's your heart? Of the seats in the red convertible Mustang story, which "condition" do you find most similar to where you are now and why?

Five

The Language of Sonship

You cannot know God the way you know anything else; you only know God spirit to Spirit, center to center, by a process of "mirroring" where like knows like and love knows love—deep calling unto deep."
– Richard Rohr

My words, they are spirit and they are life.

– Jesus

We are getting to the most fundamental, yet practical, element of the *Abba Formation*. It is about what happens when the Holy Spirit is allowed to pray, speak, and sing through us—God's Spirit working in and through the human spirit. In many ways it comes down to words, and there are three evidences that are plainly and simply "in our face" to show us the importance of words to our very life and freedom.

First, if God reveals His only Son to the world as the Word (John 1:1), it shouldn't surprise anyone that words are important to God and fundamental to who He is. He created the universe (material reality) with words (Gen. 1), He sustains all material reality with words, and He transforms what needs transforming with words (Heb. 1:3). There are literally hundreds of references to "the word of God" throughout Scripture causing us to take note that communication by words is unique to man and God (and angelic beings).

Second, James tells us that the tongue (words) directs the course of a man's life. He says it is the most unruly member of man's body, and it truly cannot be tamed without supernatural help. Our words are like the rudder of a great ship. The same way a rudder determines the direction and course of a ship, the tongue (i.e., words spoken) determine the course and direction of a man's life.

Even so the tongue is a little member and boasts great things. See how great a forest a little fire kindles! And the tongue is a fire, a world of iniquity. The tongue is so set among our members that it defiles the whole body, and sets on fire the course of nature; and it is set on fire by hell.
James 3:5-6

Finally, words are the unique vehicle through which God communicates and creates. He speaks to create a tangible, existing materiality, an incarnation of His thoughts, will and desire. He also speaks so those He has created to share the Triune joy can know Him and be known by Him. He has given man the right, responsibility, and power of communication in a way that no other part of His creation possesses.

Transformed by Words Inside and Out

That said, there is a huge difference between words that originate in God and those that originate in man. The letters and words you are reading right now are only symbols (symbols derived from our alphabet). The symbols represent sounds, and the sounds are culturally agreed ways to communicate meaning. God, however doesn't speak symbols as we do. He speaks reality. When He speaks, things are created. When He says, "Let there be light," the cosmos explodes with something not seen before. The energy which comes out of His being cannot be contained in hundreds of billions of stars, most of them larger than our sun. God's words are alive and full of power (Heb. 4:12). His words are "spirit," and they fit in our spirits. Stay with me, because these concepts are important. They will show us how the Holy Spirit works in and through us, ultimately transforming us into full sonship.

Executive consultant Tracy Goss believes that language is the only avenue one has for changing the context of the world. Although his application of language is to a psychological frame, his work will help us make a spiritual connection. He says language plays a large role in how individuals "apprehend and construct reality through the way they speak and listen."[28] This line of thought concerning language has been based upon Heidegger's work that has connected the concepts of language and "being."[29] All of that is to say that in some way, being made in God's image means sharing life at the level of language. We understand that the worlds were framed by the word of God (Heb. 11:3). This would include not only the cosmos—the macro worlds of God—but also the micro world of the heart of man.

Being made in God's image means sharing life at the level of language.

Ponder this:

The Creator of the universe has made a way to move into our inner world, which means

God's words, spoken in us and through us by the indwelling Spirit, have the power to reframe our inner world. The tongue of man (man's words) may set the course of a man's life ablaze, as James said, but when empowered by the Spirit, that same tongue can set your life toward God's greatest purposes and fulfillment. This is the *Abba Formation*.

The Language of Honor

We are a prophetic community, living not by what we see with the natural eye, but by what we know in the S/spirit. Paul said:

Therefore, from now on, we regard no one according to the flesh.
Even though we have known Christ according to the flesh
[he's referring to the original apostles who walked with Christ],
yet now we know Him thus no longer.
2 Corinthians 5:16

This is the way of the kingdom you and I live in. We spend a lot of time studying each other's strengths, weaknesses, past experiences, and "come-froms," but Paul says we are not even to know one another or judge one another according to the flesh (our past experiences and history). We've been made new. Then he goes on to say:

Therefore, if anyone is in Christ, he is a new creation; old things have passed away; behold, all things have become new.
2 Corinthians 5:17

The language of honor is about dealing with people on the basis of who they are in the Father's eyes, not our eyes. It's about calling out the reality of Who and what is in them as new creatures, whether they are living up to that reality or not.

Have you ever eavesdropped in on the conversation going on in the Trinity? What do you think Father, Son and Holy Spirit are saying when They talk about you? I assure you, it's all good. God's conversation and vocabulary about you is never about who you are not, but about who you are in the Father's purpose and what you are ordained to produce (as fruit) out of who you "be." The reason the "past" is not mentioned

The kingdom of darkness is always digging for the dirt; the kingdom of light is always digging for the gold. in our inheritance is because it is off limits to Trinitarian conversation. Our Triune God has chosen in His sovereign will to remember it no more. It's been sealed up in the Son of Man who "carried it away" in Himself.

You cannot build anything on the negative. No healthy family can be built simply on what is disallowed. No healthy church can be built upon a list of "shall-nots." No revival/renewal movement can be built on the priority of repentance of sin and guilt. It must be built on the positive redemptive acts of God—in Christ and by the Holy Spirit—which culminate in the visitations of the Spirit of God as overflow of the new reality.

A language of honor is the language of the Trinitarian conversation. A language of honor is focused upon celebrating sons and the gifts they have, not what they don't have. A language of honor puts on display the goodness and kindness of God and calls out people's destinies. You can either dig for the dirt or dig for the gold in people. The kingdom of darkness is always digging for the dirt; the kingdom of light is always digging for the gold.

The language of honor calls the mystery of a person's being out of the unknown into the known and brings it into light so that a person's mind gets washed by it. Our old orphan thinking is constantly renewed into sonship thinking by the language of the community. Jesus says:

Now are you clean through the words that I have spoken to you.
John 15:3

This is why our prophetic language is alive with edification, exhortation and comfort rather than criticism, guilt, and judgment.

The language of honor is nothing less than being invited into the Trinitarian conversation, and in that atmosphere, we have to learn how to receive honor as well as give it. Pastor Bill Johnson says, "If you don't learn how to receive honor you will never have a crown to lay at His feet." That leads us to the second distinctive of the language of sonship—the language of abundance.

The Language of Abundance

The language of abundance is about what you've already received—not what you're trying to obtain.

What you honor, you attract. This is the power of worship. When we honor the Lord with the worship of our lives, He comes in presence and power. When God comes among us and lives among us, everything He has becomes accessible. The language of abundance doesn't come from possessions or riches. In fact, if the first thought you have when you see the word "abundance" is riches and possessions, it's a pretty good sign you still have a good way to go in your orphan-to-son process.

The language of abundance isn't a tool or trick you can use to leverage God into getting you more stuff. The language of abundance is not a Gospel gimmick that guarantees an outcome if you say the right words enough times. The language of abundance is about what you've already received—not what you're trying to obtain. It comes out of an internal revelation that you are an heir of God, therefore a joint heir with Jesus Christ, and in that relationship all things are yours (Rom. 8:32; 1 Cor. 3:21).

The working out of that internal calibration is not a desire to acquire more "stuff." Quite the contrary. It releases you from the fear of not having enough, being enough, or doing enough, and actually sets you free to give your life away. Jesus said it so simply that sometimes we miss it:

Freely you have received, freely give.

Matthew 10:8

You will always have what you need to have when you need to have it. And you will always know what you need to know when you need to know it ... if you'll make the Holy Spirit your best friend.

We know the verse, but subconsciously interpret it through the lens of a wrong view of God to mean that we freely received once, and now must manage that little morsel we received freely and work it into something big. No. If you understand who God is, then you know He is infinite, overflowing, other-centered love and He cannot keep from giving Himself away (see *The Abba Foundation*). That is to say, we not only freely received once, but we are continually receiving freely, and therefore the "pantry" will never be bare!

At the lowest point in my life, He said it to me this way, "Kerry, you will always have what you need to have when you need to have it. And you will always know what you need to know when you need to know it ..." (and here's the caveat), "... if you'll make the Holy Spirit your best friend." I didn't understand at the time that, with natural strengths of ideation, intellection, learner, and strategic hardwired in me, Satan's tactic would always be to tempt me to fear about not having the information, the resources, and the ideas I would need at the right time. The Father was giving me a *rhema* word, knowing the battle I was about to fight, the same way He spoke sonship to Jesus in the Jordan River just before Jesus would be tempted in the wilderness. The Father, Son and Spirit speak the language of abundance. Isn't it hilarious to try to conceive of God as speaking anything else, since He can create galaxies and solar systems with just His word?

What happens to your thinking and desires if you know the pantry will never be bare? What if, no matter how much you give away, you turn around to look again, and the shelves are already restocked? What does your life look like if your best friend can take two fish and some bread and turn it into a feast for 15,000 people—and He loves to do it? You see, Jesus said, "You don't even have to think about the stuff ("take no thought"); your *Abba* knows what you need."

The reality is, a revelation of sonship produces a language of abundance, and you realize you don't have to own much. It's already yours. Jesus didn't own a stall full of horses and donkeys. It all belongs to Him. So, when He needed a colt to ride on He just gave the instructions, "When the owner asks you about it, just say 'The Master needs it.'"

Of course, the other thing that happens when you realize all things are yours is that you turn your heart to the mission of the Father. Our desire turns to the nations instead of ourselves. This is when the real fun begins. Sonship is ultimately about finishing the Father's unfinished business. A revelation of our inheritance as sons frees us from grasping for stuff like orphans so we can start bearing fruit in the Father's mission and purpose.

Why Heads of State Give Gifts to One Another

Have you ever wondered why heads of state give such strange gifts to one another? If you Google the idea, you find that on every continent, from ancient civilizations to the present, "dignitaries and leaders exchanged gifts to welcome, honor and cultivate beneficial diplomatic relationships. A gift of state captures the essence of a nation, chosen for its ability to exhibit pride in a unique culture and people."[30] Gifts of State may showcase traditions or display a particular wealth, for example precious stones or metals. In other words, gifts of State *display a certain feature or characteristic of that kingdom.* The gift becomes more than a mere formality. It serves as a reminder of the special relationship between the giver and receiver of the gift.

Heaven's essence is demonstrated on earth through the gifts of the Godhead, freely distributed so the whole world can "taste and see that the Lord is good."

What we should notice especially is that kings and heads of state don't give gifts on the basis of need. From a socio-economic standpoint, it's the wealthy giving to the wealthy. So, we may ask, "What's the point?" The point is relationships, association and honor.

This helps us rethink our ideas about the gifts of the Godhead—the Father's motivational gifts (Rom. 12), the Son's ministry gifts (Eph. 4), and the Spirit's manifestation gifts (1 Cor. 12). These gifts are NOT given to believers to make us somebody (e.g. "I'm a prophet," "I'm an apostle," "I have gifts of healings," and so on). Such ladder-climbing and title-wearing only reveal the orphan spirit is still at work. These gifts are given to His sons and daughters who have already been given access to the whole kingdom, to display the nature and characteristics of the Kingdom. God is a good God who gives good things to His children (Matt. 7:11), and all who come to Him can be His children. The Father's good pleasure is to give you the kingdom. Heaven's essence is demonstrated on earth through the gifts of the Godhead, freely distributed so the whole world can "taste and see that the Lord is good." To live in this atmosphere is to know sonship, which produces a language, which cultivates a culture. The language of abundance is a language of generosity—knowing what we have freely received, so we can freely give.

The Language of Affirmation

What is the difference between the language of honor and the language of affirmation? I am suggesting that the language of honor reaches into a person to speak to his God-ordained purpose, destiny, mission, and identity. By contrast, the language of affirmation is how we encourage one another in the smaller steps of day-to-day obedience and living.

The New Testament is, in many ways, a language manual that helps us learn how to converse in Trinitarian life. The conversation of the Trinity is Heaven's language, but as a colony of Heaven in the earth we are to continue to speak our "Mother tongue" in the home. In addition to Jesus' many instructions about our words such as, "It's not what goes into a man (certain foods), but what comes out of the man (his words)…," Paul gives us fifty-eight "one-anothers" that help us cultivate the language of affirmation. He says, "love one another," "admonish one another," "exhort one another," and "provoke one another to good works." This is the language of Heaven and the language of Heaven's family on earth. When this language arises out of hearts that really love one another, it has a different aroma than what is heard in the world. One is a *quid pro quo*, give to get; the other is "give no matter what you get," because that is just what sons living in the infinite Father do. When we freely receive the love of the Father, we are free to give His love away, encouraging, and affirming one another.

The Language of the Spirit

There is no greater advantage available to any people, race, or culture anywhere than the language of the Spirit. No education, pedigree, or social positioning comes close to what has been made available to sons and daughters of God who have received the overflowing fullness of the Holy Spirit. The language of the Spirit transcends any form of human communication. When the Holy Spirit gives us words that are beyond the limits of our own intelligence, beyond the limits of our native language, beyond the limits of human knowledge, we are literally operating from a different world.

I am aware that the topic of spiritual language (*glossolalia*) is at the ongoing center of debate, and in some circles, contention, though this is less and less the case as the global Church carries the Gospel message in power. It is not only with sensitivity that I approach the topic, but also with a humbled sense of boldness in both biblical and practical experience. Before we examine this language of the Spirit, allow me to (1) recommend some materials and (2) articulate biblical foundations for spiritual language.

Recommended Materials

For those who have not grown up in an environment where the Holy Spirit and spiritual language are common conversation or practice, I suggest two books that provide both theological and practical introduction in common sense terms.

First, Pastor Robert Morris' book, *The God I Never Knew*, is a good introduction into Spirit Baptism (which is fundamental to understanding The *Abba Cry*) coming from a person who was raised with a different doctrine.[31] Because of Pastor Morris' non-charismatic background, he is able to speak the language of those who, like himself, didn't grow up hearing about the internal work of the Holy Spirit in a believer's life as being something sane and practical.

The second book is Pastor Jack Hayford's *The Beauty of Spiritual Language*.[32] Pastor Hayford's book articulates the sensitivity of a statesman who has reached across many theological aisles to bring many streams together. He speaks with authority as one who lived and led through the decades of America's greatest spiritual outpouring. These two books will serve every hungry and thirsty reader with the kind of biblical depth on this topic that produces an unshakable faith and practice.

I would also humbly suggest that my book, *The Gifts of the Spirit for a New Generation*, could be helpful to explain how the gifts of the Spirit are an expression of the overflowing compassion of God, in spite of historical misunderstandings and excesses in both practice and purpose.

Biblical Foundations for Spiritual Language

Before we examine the language of the S/spirit, I also need to articulate biblical foundations for spiritual language. I understand and honor the fact that my assumptions may not be the same as yours, but I submit them to clarify where I'm coming from.

Spiritual Language Is a New Testament Practice

One of the first issues that need clarification is that spiritual language, or "prayer language" as some call it, isn't seen in the Old Testament or the Gospels for a reason. I will often have people ask, "If spiritual language

Jesus is first introduced into the public domain by John as the baptizer in the Holy Spirit. is so important, why don't we see it throughout the whole Bible?" That's a great question with a very straightforward answer: spiritual language is a byproduct of the outpouring of the Spirit, which came after Jesus' resurrection. This benefit is reserved for those who are born again—born of the Spirit. The nature of sin and death wasn't removed until Jesus died and was raised from the dead, and neither was a new spirit of righteousness imputed. In the Gospels we see that the disciples (and masses of followers) could not understand Jesus' parables, was because they didn't have a heart (or spiritual ears) to hear. They were still dead in spirit (Eph. 2:1).

The disciples weren't born again (spiritually alive) until Jesus met them in an upper room in Capernaum after His resurrection, breathed upon them and said, "Receive the Spirit" (John 20:22). They were born again in that moment. Notice, however, that Jesus told those same disciples, who had just *received* the Spirit, to go to Jerusalem and wait until they were *filled* with the Spirit (Acts 1:8). The Holy Spirit was poured out upon the Church in another upper room roughly fifty days later (Acts 2:1-4). Spiritual language is, therefore, strictly a New Testament practice. The next two chapters will articulate in more detail both the beauty and benefits of spiritual language. For now, let's look at three additional biblical foundations that bring the issues of baptism in the Holy Spirit and spiritual language to more than personal assumptions.

Jesus Is the Baptizer in the Holy Spirit

Jesus is first introduced into the public domain by John as "the baptizer in the Holy Spirit and with fire" (Matt. 3:11; Luke 3:16). God always reveals His nature and purpose through His names. The fact that Jesus is introduced as the "baptizer in the Holy Spirit" demonstrates that from the beginning God had purposed Spirit baptism as the means through which the Church would accomplish His mission.

Jesus fulfilled the words of John the Baptist when the Spirit was poured out upon the Church after His ascension. Earlier, Jesus had promised this experience to be "rivers of living water that would flow out of the believer's inner man" (John 7:37-39). This is significant to the idea of spiritual transformation as an inside-out work of the Spirit.

Peter Establishes Spiritual Language as Foundational and Normal in the Early Church

Luke records the watershed moment when the Gospel was first proclaimed to Gentiles. Peter went to Cornelius' house. Notice what took place:

> *While Peter was still speaking these words, the Holy Spirit fell upon all those who heard the word. And those of the circumcision who believed were astonished, as many as came with Peter, because the gift of the Holy Spirit had been poured out on the Gentiles also. For they heard them speak with tongues and magnify God.*
>
> Acts 10:44-46

Peter interpreted this experience of spiritual language (speaking with other tongues) not only as the fulfillment of the Father's promise for the Jews (Acts 1:8; 2:27, 38), but also as the indisputable evidence that the Gentiles had also been accepted by God (Acts 10:54; Acts 15:8). Think about this. What was so convincing to Jewish leaders that it settled the argument about the radical idea that Gentiles could be included in the Church? Peter, contrary to everything he had been raised to believe, declared to the Jewish leaders in Jerusalem that:

> *God, who knows the heart, acknowledged them by giving them the Holy Spirit, just as He did to us.*
>
> Acts 15:8

There is no stronger historical evidence for the reality of Spirit Baptism and spiritual language as foundational and normal in the early Church than the personal testimony of Peter (the current leader of the Church) and Luke's documentation of it in Acts.

Paul Encourages Spirit Fullness and Establishes Spiritual Language as a Tool for Personal Edification

Finally, Paul provided meticulous explanation of spiritual language as the way in which the Holy Spirit synchronizes the believer to the Father's will and purpose (1 Cor. 2:9-16), and the way spiritual language edifies both

Spirit Baptism was never about who gets to heaven or who is more spiritual than another. It is about turning orphans into sons.

the believer individually and the congregation corporately as a Kingdom way of life (1 Cor. 14).

Jesus told His disciples that a new day was at hand, where the Holy Spirit would move inside of the believers, not only transforming them at the point of their weakness but also empowering them to do even greater works of compassionate power (John 14:12-14). The Holy Spirit would teach them and show them things to come (John 16:13). They wouldn't have to worry about what to say at the critical moment, for "The Spirit will give you the words in that moment" (Luke 12:12). The Holy Spirit forms the words in the believer's spirit, and by those words He teaches and distributes everything the Father has given to the Son (John 16:15).

From the Day of Pentecost forward, it is evident that the experience of Pentecost was never intended to be a spiritual badge that separates one group of believers from another. Spirit Baptism was never about who gets to heaven or who is more spiritual than another. It is about turning orphans into sons—the transmission, the communication of the wholeness of God imparted into broken humans to restore them to their intended place. Those healed and empowered sons are called to take the good news to the orphan world and begin to release the Kingdom of God (His wholeness, justice, *shalom*) by His presence to all who will receive.

Receiving this promise of the Father is easy. Hear Peter's first message, when asked "How can we also receive what you have received?"

> *Then Peter said to them, "Repent, and let every one of you be baptized in the name of Jesus Christ for the remission of sins; and you shall receive the gift of the Holy Spirit. For the promise is to you and to your children, and to all who are afar off, as many as the Lord our God will call."*
>
> Acts 2:38-39

An Admonition and Two Cautions

There are numerous cultural and religious (i.e., denominational) objections to Spirit Baptism and the biblical evidence of spiritual language.

I will not burden you with a recitation and defense of those here since that has already been done elsewhere (as in the recommended resources mentioned earlier). However, an admonition and two cautions are in order.

Spirit Baptism as an experience alone does not guarantee maturity in sonship.

If the biblical (and global cultural) evidence for Spirit Baptism is as clear as I believe it is, why would any believer want anything less? Spirit Baptism is neither an ecstatic spiritual experience nor a badge of spirituality, but rather a means by which believers are transformed into the likeness of Christ and empowered for witness. Why wouldn't any sincere believer desire this gift?

Frankly, many have disdained such a partnership with the Holy Spirit because of so-called excesses they have heard about and some outright excesses due to a lack of appropriate pastoral teaching and guidance where such has been encountered. The truth is, leaders with an orphan heart will abuse power. That is to say, Spirit Baptism as an experience alone does not guarantee maturity in sonship. Like Simon the sorcerer (Acts 8), orphan leaders crave power to fill the identity hole in their souls. This, however, doesn't negate the validity of the experience, as evidenced by the apostles' determination to see the entire city of Samaria receive what they were lacking in their new faith. There is some statement about "babies and bathwater" that is pertinent here.

As a caution, it needs to be said that we don't get to decide what is "weird." Peter's testimony to the Jerusalem leaders boiled down to this:

> *I know this is different than anything we have ever seen. We didn't anticipate this even though, now that we reflect back, we know that Jesus had told us about it. It feels weird to us, but evidently it is not weird to God. Only He gets to decide what is weird.*
> Acts 15:7-11 (my paraphrase)

For those who argue that "if we can't find that experience in the Bible it can't be God," then consider that the Jerusalem Church had never seen tongues of fire sitting on people's heads, nor people speaking languages they hadn't learned! Peter had never seen the Holy Spirit poured out on Gentiles before, and yet he was able to find an Old Testament promise (though not necessarily precedent) to validate that what he was seeing

Consider that God is gracious to give us promises, but not required to show precedent. was from God. Consider that God is gracious to give us promises, but not required to show precedent, which leads to a relational caution.

If Spirit Baptism is neither a guarantee nor sign of spiritual maturity, we should be careful not to stand in judgment over other people's experiences, even if their experiences sound "weird" to us. Sometimes what people call a "manifestation" is merely one person's way of reacting to power. God forbid, but if ten of us accidentally got a hold of some electrical current, chances are there would be a variety of ways we would react! Just because we react differently doesn't mean each experienced a different kind of current. So, let's give each other room to be different. The Lord has been pretty clear through Paul's writings to Corinth about what is distracting, self-promoting, or just plain selfish.

In short, our spiritual experiences should always be measured by how they draw us closer to the grace of Jesus, the personal fellowship of the Holy Spirit, and a desire to bless others. The danger is that our spiritual experiences can become stepping stones to our own self-exaltation— "Look at me! God talked to me!" In fact, you should be walking with the Holy Spirit in such a way that you have many experiences and many conversations—including some that are too private and intimate to share with others (As both Paul and John saw things by the Holy Spirit that were "unlawful to utter").

If your spiritual encounter does not bond you with the Holy Spirit, the earthly resident member of the Godhead, and make you more like Jesus in loving others, it could be said that you have just had a personal experience, and perhaps a huge distraction at that. Nevertheless, even if an entire generation were to get it wrong or totally ignore the ministry of the Spirit, that doesn't nullify its reality, validity, or availability to others.

What Have We Said?

Sonship has its own language—a language of royalty and honor.
Sonship communicates in the language of abundance.
Sonship communicates in the language of affirmation.
Sonship communicates in the language of the supernatural: Spirit to spirit.

God's words, spoken in us and through us by the indwelling Spirit, have the power to reframe our inner world.

The language of the Spirit has strong biblical foundations that should not be denied simply because of negative experiences.

PRAYER

Heavenly Father, my Abba, You have not given me a spirit of bondage again to fear but a spirit of adoption that cries "Abba, Father." This language of the Spirit opens my spirit to the world and ways of Heaven. Holy Spirit, I welcome You to form in me the language of honor, the language of abundance, the language of affirmation, and the language of the Spirit. I ask You, Lord Jesus, to fill me (again) right now with the Holy Spirit. I want everything You have for me today. I know that every good gift comes from You. Holy Spirit, thank You for making the words of my mouth consistent with Your words. Thank You for using me to make Heaven available everywhere I go. In the name and realm of the Father, Son, and Holy Spirit. Amen.

GROUP DISCUSSION

1. What are the three "in our face" evidences that show us the importance of words to our very life and freedom?

2. What is the *language of honor*, and where does it come from?

3. What is the *language of abundance*, and how is it different from our carnal notions of getting rich?

4. What is the *language of affirmation*, and how is it different from the language of honor?

5. What are the three biblical anchors that establish the *language of the Spirit* as normative for the New Testament Church?

6. What questions does this raise for you about how the Spirit shapes the culture of the Church as the colony of Heaven? Any other questions?

Six

The "Active Ingredient" for Transformation

What if the miracle of spiritual formation is not that the Holy Spirit overrides our habits, but that He empowers us from within to form new, life-giving ones?

– Glenn Packiam

If you read the label closely, whether medicines or cleansers, you will find an "active ingredient" that targets the problem. The rest is mostly talc or chalk. When it comes to our transformation, much of what we call "spiritual disciplines" turns out to be talc, unless the Holy Spirit is present. The Holy Spirit is the active ingredient in your personal transformation. Paul says:

We ... are being transformed into the same image from glory to glory, just as by the Spirit of the Lord.

2 Corinthians 3:18

Isn't it interesting that Paul could say so clearly, so plainly, so to the point, that transformation comes "by the Spirit of the Lord," and yet we try every other way possible to produce change in our own lives and ignore a daily, intentional relationship with the Holy Spirit? A real experience with Him will create a noticeable difference in your conduct, behavior, attitudes, ambitions, and even the words that flow out of your mouth.

The Holy Spirit does not want His power and blessing to mesmerize or entertain you (though if we need to be entertained, it beats the frequent alternatives). He doesn't do sign-and-wonder shows to fulfill our fascination. The Holy Spirit has an assignment, and Jesus tells us what it is. He says:

When He, the Spirit of truth, has come, He will guide you into all truth; for He will not speak on His own authority, but whatever He hears He will speak; and He will tell you things to come. He will glorify Me, for He will take of what is Mine and declare it to you.

John 16:13-14

The three primary objectives of the Holy Spirit as it relates to believers are:

1. **To bear witness of your sonship.** The case I am making in *The Abba Factor* and *The Abba Formation* is simply this, that Jesus has come to bring many sons to glory (Heb. 2:10), and it is the internal, tenacious work of the Spirit of adoption—the Holy Spirit—that is delivering us from the tyranny of the orphan spirit and revealing to us the reality that we are sons.

2. **To lead and guide you into all truth.** The transforming agent replaces the lies that you have believed with the truth about both Him and yourself. This includes convicting of sin, shining a light via the conscience —the voice of your spirit—on behaviors that are no longer consistent with a son's new nature in Christ. A clarification on this point is necessary. Allow me to use my personal story to explain.

I was reared in a very Christ-centered, Spirit-centered home and church life. The Holy Spirit was not peripheral, but central to the teachings I heard and the modeling of ministry that I saw. Unfortunately, some of my religious upbringing caused my understanding of the Holy Spirit's role to convict me of sin to be distorted. (In *The Abba Foundation* we explain that our view of God shapes all our understanding of how He relates to us, whether this view is informed by the life and lens of Jesus, or by our own religious misunderstanding and life experiences.) I saw the Holy Spirit as a type of neighborhood KGB informant who would notify God when I messed up. Now, I know that God went to extreme measures to deal with my sin in His Son, so that I can enjoy God as the loving Father that He is. Yes, the Holy Spirit does convict me of sin, but it is not out of a punitive motivation. He is with me and for me. He doesn't scold me when I act contrary to my new nature any more than I would scold one of my children, should they take a tumble when they are learning to walk. That's not to say I haven't had the Lord speak very sobering words to me—I have—but never with an edge of condemnation, shame, or hint of anything but love. The Holy Spirit convicts us of sin as part of His transforming work in us, to lead and guide us into all truth.

3. **To endue (clothe, fill) you with power.** He does this to enable you to do the works of Jesus (Acts 1:8; John 14:12-14). Ultimately, the internal work must become a missional work focused on the Father's unfinished business in a broken world. It's not just about you. (I will explain this in the final chapters.)

The point is, everything God has made available to you, by the Holy Spirit, is to bring you into a fully transformed experience in the life and fellowship of the Trinity. As mentioned earlier, there is no greater tool for us to partner with the Holy Spirit in this process of transformation than the exercise of spiritual language. No amount of human effort comes close to what has been made available to us by the overflowing fullness of the Spirit. Through spiritual language, the Holy Spirit gives us words that transcend the limitations of our mind. This is such an important piece of our transformation that we need to spend some time on it.

A Spiritual Partnership

Before we explore the beauty and benefits of spiritual language, let's underscore the necessity of partnership in the transformation process. First is the partnership between *Abba* and the Holy Spirit. The Father has encoded you with gifts and callings, but it is the Holy Spirit who searches the "deep things" of the Father about you. It is by the partnership between Father and Spirit that your callings are revealed to you. Then, there is also a partnership between us and the Holy Spirit. He does His part, but only to the degree that we allow Him to work in and through us. How do we cooperate with the Holy Spirit to decode our code?

1. **Pray it out.** Praying in the Spirit is tapping into the mysteries (1 Cor. 14:2, 4). This involves a daily discipline to make prayer language a regular part of your life. It also means simply maintaining an ongoing conversation with God about what He wants to do in your life. One of the best ways to pray it out is simply to ask the Father, "What do You want me to ask You for?"

2. **Play it out.** Do what is in front of you. It is difficult to turn a car that is not moving. In the same way, it will be easier for the Holy Spirit to turn

you, transform you, or redirect you if you are doing something with what He has said to you. If that doesn't seem to be a fit, do something else. You will find a place where your gift makes room for you. That is to say, the internal wiring of the Father makes it easier for you to do certain things than others. It's what you were made to do. Keep playing it out until you find your niche and the grace that accompanies God's call on your life.

3. **Say it out.** Declare what He has said about you and to you. "I [God] have said ... so that you may boldly say ..." (Heb. 13:5-6). Paul declares that he will pray in the S/spirit and pray in his known language (the understanding) also (1 Cor. 14:15). There are multiple ways to declare what the Holy Spirit is saying and doing in us, but speaking those things out keeps us focused on what He is doing in us now. Spiritual language will help you keep your head above the fray of orphan thinking and public opinion. The *Abba Cry* will allow you to see, think, and feel from His perspective.

Why the Emphasis on Spiritual Language?

Let's look again at 1 Corinthians 2 and consider what Paul says about how the Holy Spirit uses words:

> *These things we also speak, not in words which man's wisdom*
> *teaches but which the Holy Spirit teaches,*
> *comparing spiritual things with spiritual.*
> 1 Corinthians 2:13

The emphasis on "words" seems to point to the words the Spirit *uses*, and not just what the Spirit *teaches*. It indicates that He uses certain words, a vocabulary of the S/spirit. Gordon Fee, in his monumental work on Paul's understanding of the Holy Spirit, asserts that it would have been much easier for Paul to say anything else, especially because this emphasis could have reinforced the very problem he was trying to resolve. Paul was addressing the Corinthian's belief that, since they had so many ecstatic experiences through inspired utterances, they had achieved some secret gnostic elevation (up the ladder of deification).[33] They greatly valued spiritual language but were misusing it for personal gain. Though it was risky, Paul didn't shy away from expressing the value of the Spirit's words, but he brought a needed clarification that it is the Spirit who speaks—it is He who forms the words—so we can take no pride in spiritual language or what it produces, as if it was our own doing.

This partnership between the yielded believer and the Holy Spirit can be observed scientifically. Dr. Caroline Leaf, neurological researcher on brain function, says:

> When we pray consciously there is a firing up of the frontal lobe. However, when you pray in tongues the activity of the frontal lobe quietens down completely, which shows the Holy Spirit is actively forming the words, doing the praying, not your mind, but in your spirit .... Brain scans reveal that the actual forming of the words is coming from somewhere else.[34]

Recent research in the University of Pennsylvania has shown that while the subjects of the study spoke in tongues:

> ... their frontal lobes—the thinking, willful part of the brain through which people control what they do—were relatively quiet, as were the language centers ... The regions that are involved in maintaining self-consciousness were active: The women were not in a blind trance.[35]

This is to say that spiritual language is formed by the Holy Spirit in the human spirit, not in the mind.

Pastor Jack Hayford, pastor, notable author, and founder of The King's University, asserts that the experience is spiritual in nature, as the believer surrenders to God, but this surrender is not to the point of "succumbing to some state of mindless oblivion." [36] David Kling further explains that it is a non-rational experience that involves the suspension of the ordinary rational process, allowing the believer to have a spontaneous and wondrous encounter with God through the Spirit.[37]

Is this a new discovery? Not at all. Paul had already explained this supernatural partnership in the same letter to the Corinthians. He says:

Spiritual Language is available to every believer.

For he who speaks in a tongue does not speak to men but to God, ... however, in the S/spirit he speaks mysteries.

1 Corinthians 14:2

When we put the two together we can see that the way the Spirit of God synchronizes our spirits with God's plans and purposes comes about through spiritual language—certainly in a way that our minds cannot understand, and perhaps most importantly, not in a way in which we can take any credit. By Paul's record, spiritual language is significant to our transformation. It is both beautiful and beneficial, as we shall now see.

The Beauty of Spiritual Language

1. Spiritual Language is available to every believer.

*Repent, be baptized in the name of the Lord Jesus,
and you shall receive the gift of the Holy Spirit. For this promise
is <u>for you and your children, and to all that are afar off,
even as many as the Lord our God shall call</u>.*

Acts 2:38-39

The beauty of this avenue of Holy Spirit acceleration is that it is available for all who believe and receive the Spirit's fullness. This was evident on the Day of Pentecost.

And they were all filled with the Holy Spirit and began to speak with other tongues, as the Spirit gave them utterance.

Acts 2:4

Understand that in Luke's writing—both in his Gospel and in Acts— chapters one and two function as the lens through which we interpret the rest of the book. In the same way, Acts becomes the lens through which we interpret the epistles.[38]

Think about how wonderful it is that this gift is so inclusive—it is fully available to every believer. In our human experience, those things that are deemed most essential are usually available to an exclusive few. Higher education is available to those who have good grades, time, and money. Sometimes it seems the most coveted positions are available only to those who have the right connections. Many would say that wealth is available to those who are born in the right country or class. However, the power of transformation by the indwelling Holy Spirit (and spiritual language) is available to every believer as the Spirit prays through the believer's spirit. This is a sure sign of the Gospel message—it is never exclusive for a few, but freely given to "whosoever will" (Acts 2:39).

2. Spiritual Language is available to you 24/7.

The experience of spiritual language is not limited to a super-charged atmosphere—when the music is right, the lighting is right, and the right person is speaking at church. Notice what Paul says:

> *What is the conclusion then? I will pray with the spirit, and I will also pray with the understanding. I will sing with the spirit, and I will also sing with the understanding. … And the spirits of the prophets are subject to the prophets.*
> 1 Corinthians 14:15, 32

Paul is telling us that the Holy Spirit is not so temperamental that He only works if the mood is just right. The Holy Spirit is in you and will never leave you. The good news is that He is always "on." He is not moody or hypersensitive as we've made Him out to be.

Let me illustrate the power of availability. I travel to Bogota, Colombia, quite often because my wife is Colombian. It's a beautiful nation with beautiful, gracious, and happy people. Socio-economically and culturally it is poorer in some ways and richer in some ways than how I grew up. One of the ways it is richer, in addition to great family values, is that many things that we consider luxuries in the U.S. are quite affordable there. For example, we have had the "luxury" of hiring a car and driver for a day, who is ready whenever we ask him to drive us anywhere we want to go. Now think about having a driver sitting in your car all day, every day, waiting for you to give him instructions of **Spiritual** when and where you want to go. **Language**

I am not saying that the Holy Spirit is our chauffeur. **is available** He is not my bellhop, chauffeur, or errand boy. He is **to you 24/7.**

107

Spiritual Language is a tangible, physical witness that God is living inside you. God. However, I am trying to paint a picture for you of what it is like for the Holy Spirit to be available to you 24/7. What I am saying to you is that by spiritual language, the Holy Spirit is readily available, at your will, to pray through you and release in you the mind of God, disclosing to you the deep things of God. If God directs, you can get anywhere in the world you need to go, any time you want to go there! You can pray for things your natural mind knows nothing about (Rom. 8:26-27). Whether you're in a good mood or feeling disconnected, rich or poor, a frequent flyer or bedfast, you have direct and ready access to the plans and purposes of God by the Holy Spirit who lives in you.

3. Spiritual Language is a tangible, physical witness that God is living inside you.

Research done on hundreds of Spirit-filled believers found that those who regularly practice glossolalia have an abiding sense that God is in them and always with them (The Greek word *glossolalia* refers to speaking in unknown tongues). Therefore, they are typically less depressed than non-*glossolalists*. The research goes on to say that those who pray in the Spirit have an abiding sense of God's presence and a confidence that "the cupboard will never be bare."[39]

This might be a new thought for you. Are you battling depression? Pray in the Spirit. These rivers of living water will wash out the debris of the soul and turn your attention to others.

This awareness of God's presence in your life is also powerful when you are facing temptation. Your thoughts, passions, and the desires of the flesh seem very powerful because they reside within you. They feel so real that the memory banks of the "old man" scream through your flesh, "These desires are really you!" However, when you pray in the Spirit, you are reminded, beyond the shadow of a doubt, that the Holy Spirit dwells in you. Spiritual language pours like rivers out of your innermost being to say, "No, the old man has been crucified with Christ. You are dead to sin but alive to God!"

Spiritual language increases your love for others. 4. **Spiritual language increases your love for others.**

Paul reveals the fundamentally radical revolution of the new humanity in Christ when he declares,

The love of God has been poured out in our hearts by the Holy Spirit who was given to us.

Romans 5:5

Spiritual language is the key to Christlikeness.

This changes everything. The motivations, the "want-tos," the heart desires at the root of everything else are changed by the indwelling Holy Spirit. The Holy Spirit is not primarily given to make you feel bad when you sin (though you will). The Holy Spirit is not primarily given to you to give you a powerful ministry (though you won't have one without Him). The Holy Spirit is pouring out, overflowing the infinite love of God in our spirits, and it changes our perspective, our purpose, our expectation, and our identity. When I live from an inside-out-overflow of God's love, I am no longer living for myself—what I can get, what I can control, or what I can become. There is a very practical side to this.

This is not some ethereal pie-in-the-sky daydream, "Can't we all just get along?" This is the real work of the Holy Spirit in your spirit and mine, changing attitudes about others who are not like us, and causing us to fall in love with people we have been taught to hate. However, it doesn't happen automatically or incidentally, does it? We all know many Christians who have the Holy Spirit in them but are still prejudiced, vengeful, bigoted and don't sound very Christlike. What makes the difference?

It comes down to yielding ourselves to the presence of the Spirit. The more room we will give the Holy Spirit in life and conversation, the more we will look, think, and act like Jesus. You can know when you're not "filled to overflowing" when others don't look so good to you, when their voice gets on your nerves, or when there is increased friction in relationships. A friend of mine said recently, "I thought I was spiritual, but now I realize I had just been alone. When I was forced to be with people, other things started coming to the surface."

5. Spiritual language is the key to Christlikeness.

Spiritual language is the time-release capsule of the nature of God at the deepest place of your being, which shapes everything else.

The carpenter's rule is to "measure twice, cut once." The precision that is necessary for fine craftsmanship requires that the same measure be applied at every cut. I learned many years ago in woodworking class that even if you are building something as crude as a wood shed or a patio

Herein lies both the challenge and genius of Christianity. form, you never, ever use the piece that you just cut as the measure for the next piece. If you do, each piece of wood gets increasingly longer (though in small increments) and in short order you are off by an inch or more. Good craftsmanship demands that every piece of wood must be cut by the original measure, not a copy. There can only be one original measure. In terms of spiritual maturity, Jesus is the original measure.

Years ago, when we used cassette tapes to reproduce church teachings, we would insert a "quality guarantee" statement with each cassette that said, "If this cassette is defective please call such-and-such number for a replacement." On occasion we would receive several returns of the same message and realized it wasn't the copy that was defective, but the master. You can't correct the problem if the master is bad. The same is true for mistakes in architectural drawings, engineering specs or skyscraper designs. If the master plan is bad, the finished product will be bad.

Herein lies both the challenge and genius of Christianity. We know that Jesus made twelve disciples (and one of those guys didn't make it), and those eleven made many more disciples, and then those made more, and so on, for a couple of millennia. From a human perspective, it would be natural to ask, "How many inches (or miles) are we off from the original blueprint as given to us in Christ?" That could be a problem if each disciple was reproducing his own, slightly modified, personal version of Christianity. However, the reality and genius are this: included in Jesus' last command to His original disciples was a promise:

Behold, I send the Promise of My Father upon you; but tarry in the city of Jerusalem until you are endued with power from on high.

Luke 24:49

The indwelling Holy Spirit is the guarantee that every believer can be discipled to Jesus himself (by the Holy Spirit). The indwelling Holy Spirit is the guarantee that every believer can be discipled to Jesus himself (by the Holy Spirit). Jesus guaranteed it when He said:

And I will pray the Father,
and He will give you <u>another</u> Helper,
that He may abide with you forever.

John 14:16

110

The Greek expression translated "another Helper" is *allon parakletos*, meaning *"just like me in every way."*

Spiritual language accelerates your awareness of sonship.

You are not a disciple of your pastor, your bishop, or your apostle. You are a disciple of Jesus Christ, and the indwelling Holy Spirit is ensuring that you are a copy of the Master, not the copy of a copy. In other words, you are not a "knockoff" Christian.

As you learn to partner with the indwelling Holy Spirit through spiritual language, the Holy Spirit forms Christ in you and transforms you into the likeness of Christ. The Holy Spirit knows how the Father hardwired you. He knows every trauma, wound, rejection, and slightly distorted idea that has marked your life. He also knows how to navigate every one of those speed bumps to make mid-course corrections in you so that you grow up in the knowledge of Christ, not in the knowledge of your own version of the Gospel.

Let's make one final connection. Jude says,

> *Now to Him who is able to keep you from stumbling,*
> *And to present you faultless Before the presence*
> *of His glory with exceeding joy ….*
>
> Jude 1:24

Notice, however, that this is preceded by the exhortation to …

> *… Build yourself up on your most holy faith, praying in the Holy Spirit.*
>
> Jude 1:20

The two are not disconnected. The more you activate your partnership with the Holy Spirit via your prayer language, the truer to the course, the more accurate each cut, the more quickly and clearly you reflect the glory of God as a disciple of Jesus because the Holy Spirit is activated to do the work.

6. Spiritual language accelerates your awareness of sonship.

When a believer prays in the spirit, the mind is "unfruitful," neither producing the language nor in charge of the process. This feels like a loss of control at first, and we must enter a deeper level of trust in God in practical ways. However, it is in this very place where we learn to listen to the heart instead of the head. The "knower" (man's spirit), by the Holy Spirit, will be articulating who you are in God, as a son of God.

For as many as are led by the Spirit of God, these are sons of God. For you did not receive the spirit of bondage again to fear, but you received the Spirit of adoption by whom we cry out, " Abba, Father." The Spirit Himself bears witness with our spirit that we are children of God.

Romans 8:14-16

Your mind will keep replaying the old scripts based on past experiences and the enemy's interpretation of those events, but the Spirit is tenacious in forming the "*Abba Cry*" in our spirits.

Because you are sons, God has sent forth the Spirit of His Son into your hearts, crying out, "Abba, Father!" Therefore you are no longer a slave but a son, and if a son, then an heir of God through Christ.

Galatians 4:6-7

The sooner we give ourselves to trusting the work and words of the Spirit, the sooner we get locked into the reality of who we really are. The Spirit of God within your spirit is crying "Daddy!" which recalibrates your sense of sonship.

Picture a window with the shade pulled down, and on the other side of the window is the eternal, or spiritual, realm. Through the words that come by the Spirit, we get glimpses into that realm. Imagine the Holy Spirit raising the shade to where we can see and know what we are unable to see and know any other way. Then imagine if this shade was being raised and lowered constantly and the only way to see out the window was to get in sync with this frequency. That is what these "words" from the Holy Spirit help us do. We touch the divine frequency, the eternal realm, the mind of the Spirit, and get glimpses into the Father's mind, will and purpose for us so that we can cooperate with it.

We have touched on the importance and the beauty of spiritual language. We will devote the next chapter to explore the many benefits of this partnership with the Holy Spirit through S/spirit-initiated language.

What Have We Said?

The Holy Spirit is the active ingredient in our personal transformations.

The Holy Spirit's mission is to bear witness of our sonship, lead and guide us into all truth (including what's true about ourselves and others), and fill us with power.

Transformation involves a partnership in which we cooperate with the internal work of the Holy Spirit in our lives. We cooperate by praying it out, playing it out, and saying it out.

The Holy Spirit synchronizes our spirits with God's plans and purposes through spiritual language.

The beauty of spiritual language is that it is available to every believer at all times.

The beauty of spiritual language is that it is a physical, tangible witness that God lives inside of me by the Spirit.

The beauty of spiritual language is that it increases our love for others.

The beauty of spiritual language is that it is a key to Christlikeness.

The Spirit ensures that I am not a copy of a copy, but a copy of the original—a disciple of Jesus himself. The same Spirit that was in Jesus is in me.

The beauty of spiritual language is that it accelerates our awareness of sonship.

PRAYER

Father, I thank You that You were never willing to remain removed from us. You weren't willing to stay removed in Heaven, in a box called the Ark of the Covenant, or behind a veil in the Holiest of Holies. Thank You that You sent Your Son who put on flesh and came to dwell with us as Immanuel. Thank You, Jesus, that You did not shrink back from the shame and pain of humanity. I'm especially thankful, Lord Jesus, that You weren't content to be with only a few but sent Your Holy Spirit, not just to be with us, but in us. I receive You, Holy Spirit and I want everything You have for me. I invite You to continue to convince me of my sonship, convict and convince me of my new nature, lead and guide me into all truth, and fill and clothe me (inside and out) with power to be a witness. Holy Spirit, I invite

You to speak to me today, and even tonight while I sleep. Train my thoughts in the night season. In the name and realm of the Father, Son, and Holy Spirit. Amen.

GROUP DISCUSSION

1. What have been some of your preconceived notions of the Holy Spirit? Law-enforcer? KGB informant? Distant and unknowable? Other? Please explain.

2. Why is it important to be a disciple of Jesus rather than a disciple of a disciple of Jesus?

3. Think about the difference between trying to serve the Lord if His presence only resides in a box in Jerusalem, or behind a curtain in the Temple, or even down at the building of your local church, versus having Him in you everywhere you go. List some advantages or disadvantages.

4. Which of the six aspects of the beauty of spiritual language seem most important to you?

Seven

The Benefits of Praying in the Spirit

*To see it clearly is to grasp the complete desirability of such
a resource of prayer for anyone.*

— Jack Hayford

We all have a life message—something God has done in us, taught us, or we have uniquely experienced in such a way that it becomes a theme of our life in impacting others. The benefits of Spiritual language—the *Abba Cry*—is one of those key themes in my life. *By praying in the Spirit,* I specifically mean praying or speaking from my spirit by the Holy Spirit, in a language that my mind has not learned (Acts 2:1-4; 1 Cor. 14:14-15). It is a deep conviction of mine that if believers could glimpse the potential benefits of this partnership with the Holy Spirit, there would be little need or desire for the many substitutes to which we give ourselves in the quest for excellence or fulfillment. Consider these:

1. Spiritual Language immediately includes you in the ongoing conversation of the Trinity.

God is a personal God—three persons, yet one essence. Therefore, it shouldn't surprise us that the Father, Son, and Holy Spirit talk with one another. Notice how Scripture reveals Their conversation. Listen to what Father, Son and Holy Spirit are saying to and about each other:

The Lord said to my Lord,
"Sit at My right hand,
Till I make Your enemies Your footstool."
The Lord shall send the rod of Your strength out of Zion.
Rule in the midst of Your enemies!
The Lord has sworn and will not relent,
"You are a priest forever according to the order of
Melchizedek."

Psalm 110:1-2,4

Spiritual Language immediately includes you in the ongoing conversation of the Trinity.

115

And suddenly a voice came from heaven, saying, "This is My beloved Son, in whom I am well pleased."

Matthew 3:17

So Jesus said to him, "Why do you call Me good? No one is good but One, that is, God."

Mark 10:18

That's the conversation of the Trinity.

Notice, however, that their conversation also includes the Father's thoughts about us. Jesus says He will declare to the Holy Spirit what the Father has declared to Him, and ...

He [the Holy Spirit] will take those things of mine [Jesus] and reveal them unto you ... all things the Father has are mine.

John 16:15

This is good news! All that the Father has, He has given to Jesus, and Jesus says that the Holy Spirit will take those things (all things) and reveal them to us. Think about that.

God reveals His deep things to us by the Holy Spirit, who searches out the deep things of the Father (about you and others) and reveals them (declares and discloses them) to you. God is not downloading His thoughts to your head (your thinker).

For My thoughts are not your thoughts,
Nor are your ways My ways," says the LORD.
"For as the heavens are higher than the earth,
So are My ways higher than your ways,
And My thoughts than your thoughts

Isaiah 55:8-9

Instead, the Father reveals His thoughts about you to your spirit (your knower), by spiritual language.

These things God has revealed to us through the Spirit ... And we impart this in words not taught by human wisdom but taught by the Spirit, interpreting spiritual truths to those who are spiritual. The

*natural person does not accept the things of the Spirit of God, for they
are folly to him, and he is not able to understand them because they
are spiritually discerned.*

1 Corinthians 2:10-14 (ESV)

You are included in the conversation God is having about you! How do
you get in on that conversation? Through spiritual language.

2. Spiritual language enables communication with God that bypasses the limits of the mind.

Paul says:

*If a man prays in an unknown tongue he is not speaking to men,
but to God.*

1 Corinthians 14:2

This is an unimaginable benefit because our minds have very limited
information about everything that needs to be done, not only in the
immediate need, but in all of the eventual and peripheral impacts that
must occur. Let me share a couple of examples.

A couple of years ago, my wife (Chiqui) and I were having our
customary time with the Lord to usher in the New Year. It was the end
of a good and fruitful year, and we were very happy where we were in our
lives and ministries. We were living well within our means in a comfortable
condo that required no yard work. We had no thought of any changes we
wanted to make in the near future. During Chiqui's prayer time she asked
the Father her customary, "*Abba*, what do You want to give me this year
that You want me to ask You for?" (It's a good way to pray). For the prior
three New Year's Eves, that had been a significant conversation between
Chiqui and the Father, so she was excitedly anticipating to hear what He
would disclose to her. She started praying in the Spirit and writing what
she sensed God was saying. The Lord spoke two or three things, including
something about "a new house." It was so far off our radar that she didn't
even write it down or mention it to me. Her mind kicked it out. Then just
a few minutes later, as we were concluding our prayer time, I began to pray
in English after having prayed for a while in the Spirit. I heard myself say,
"And Lord, thank You for the new house You are going to give us."

Praying in the S/spirit will fast forward the plans of God for your life. We both looked at each other in shock. It was not in our minds nor our perceivable personal interest. Eight months later, we were moving into a new home, which the Lord has used to be a blessing to many. It was praying in the S/spirit and then getting God's purposes on our own radar that fast-forwarded what the Lord had planned. *Praying in the S/spirit will fast forward the plans of God for your life.*

Here is another example. A pastor friend of mine shared a story about his sister. She was praying in the Spirit when a sense of urgency came over her. She prayed with intensity and heard three names and a word: "undamaged." The thoughts came so clearly, through what was a fairly common practice for her, that she wrote down the three names and the word in her prayer journal. That same evening, she took a wrong turn in a complicated intersection and was broadsided in the driver's side door by a UPS tractor-trailer freight truck. The freight driver climbed out of the cab expecting to find the car crushed under the huge tires of his truck. To his shock, he found that after such a violent collision neither his truck nor the car he had T-boned had a dent or even a scratch! The woman, slightly shaken, emerged from the car without a scratch or bruise. When the police arrived a few minutes later they said, "We thought there was an accident here. Wasn't there a collision?"

My friend's sister went home and immediately went to her prayer journal. The three names she had heard from her spirit (by the Holy Spirit) were the names of the two officers that arrived on the scene and the investigating officer who filed the "non-report." Of course, the word "undamaged" had new meaning to her.

Through her daily practice of praying in the S/spirit, the Holy Spirit had both interceded for this situation in advance (a benefit we will discuss next) and revealed to her enough of the details in advance so that she would know where her salvation came from and gave her a "glory story" to tell. He wants to do the same for you.

Jesus said that He would send the Holy Spirit to live, not just "with" but "in" the believer, to teach us all things, lead and guide us into all truth, and *show us things to come* (John 16:13). That is to say, the believer who lives by the Spirit isn't limited to knowledge that is physical or empirical in nature. The realities of the spiritual, rational and physical dimensions are all available to the believer who learns to partner with the Holy Spirit.

Sometimes the Lord gives us insight to spare us from tragedy, and if we are attentive to His prompting, there's no story to tell. When I was a youth pastor, the girl I was dating in college had invited me to come to her parents' home and spend the Fourth of July holiday weekend. It sounded like a good plan until a couple of mornings prior

How often the Holy Spirit tries to warn us of impending trouble but we're not paying attention.

to the weekend I was praying in the S/spirit and had a strange sense of foreboding in my spirit about the trip. As I continued to pray, the more my mind warred against my spirit, "You can't tell her you're not coming; it may ruin your relationship, she may misinterpret it, what a hassle." However, the sense of warning in my spirit was so clear that I called her and told her about it, and that I wouldn't be coming. No, she didn't understand. Yes, it was a hassle. But the relationship survived and the only story I have to tell about that weekend is that nothing happened. That's my "glory story" from that weekend. Nothing happened, and I'm alive to tell about it.

Think about these two stories. My friend's sister was able to walk away from a premature death because she learned to partner with the Holy Spirit through spiritual language. My story is that I never had an accident or tragedy that Fourth of July weekend at all. The Father's will and purpose for His children is that life would go well with us, and we would live until we are satisfied and fulfilled in purpose. This begs a question. We often hear of believers experiencing horrible tragedies and even premature death (and there is no simple formula or guarantee of invincibility), so we must wonder how often the Holy Spirit tries to warn us of impending trouble but we're not paying attention or have not learned how to tap into the plans and purposes of God on a daily basis.

3. Spiritual Language enables us to pray accurately, according to God's will.

Have you ever wondered how to pray according to God's will? Paul tells us that our infirmity or weakness in prayer is that we don't know how to pray as we should.

Spiritual Language enables us to pray accurately, according to God's will.

Likewise the Spirit also helps in our weaknesses. For we do not know what we should pray for as we ought,
Romans 8:26

We don't know what to ask for, and even if we know the what, we may not know exactly how God wants to bring it about. Paul, however, gives us the good news. There is a way we can pray perfectly and accurately, according to God's will. He explains:

> *For we do not know what we should pray for as we ought,*
> *but the Spirit Himself makes intercession for us with groanings*
> *which cannot be uttered. Now He who searches the hearts knows*
> *what the mind of the Spirit is, because He makes intercession*
> *for the saints according to the will of God.*
> Romans 8:26-27

The Spirit makes intercession for us. The beauty of spiritual language is that when we don't know how to think or how to pray about a situation, the Holy Spirit knows exactly what the will of God is, and prays that through us.

A few years ago my wife woke up very early one morning (very unusual for her since she is not a morning person). She was so awake, though, that she knew the Holy Spirit was prompting her. She felt an urgency to pray but didn't know what to pray for, so she prayed in the Spirit for a couple of hours. She continued praying while she got ready for work and for most of her hour-long commute to work.

She was traveling on IH-10 into the Galleria district of Houston, where she worked at the time. As is common in that particular intersection during rush hour, traffic came to a standstill in the exit lane. Chiqui looked in her rear-view mirror and saw a Mac Truck coming behind her at a high rate of speed. Her reaction was to cry, "Jesus!!!" She regained consciousness a few minutes later. Her car had been hit from behind and then spun across two more lanes of fast-moving traffic, coming to rest on the right shoulder. The car was a crumpled mess of metal, but Chiqui walked out of it with a few bruises and scratches. Could it be that the Holy Spirit had been praying through her for her own protection that morning? Though we don't know exactly how, we are assured of God's intervention and protection.

Another aspect of prayer to which this applies is in our praying for people or nations. As sons of God and partners in His mission, we are called to intercede far beyond the concerns of our inner circle. Paul says:

Therefore I exhort first of all that supplications, prayers, intercessions, and giving of thanks be made for all men, for kings and all who are in authority, that we may lead a quiet and peaceable life in all godliness and reverence.
1 Timothy 2:1

Spiritual language is a primary way that God downloads His will and purposes for your life.

How do we pray accurately for "all men"? I must confess that my thoughts about ISIS are very different from God's thoughts. Mine are mixed with national, ethnic and political biases. In my not-so-spiritual-moments, I would deal with all the lifetime politicians first, then I would go wipe ISIS off the map. Admittedly, that's a purely earthly, nationalistic, ungodly mindset. God's thoughts are vastly different. God knows that there is a Saul of Tarsus in that group, watching his own brothers, but troubled with what he sees. God knows how to reach through the hatred and biases they have been raised in, and He loves them the same way He loves me, the same way He loves Jesus. If I get in the middle of the Trinitarian Conversation and start to listen—really listen—I will catch the Father's heart for those whom I may assume are the most unlovable people of the world!

4. Spiritual language is a primary way that God downloads His will and purposes for your life.

God is moving at light speed and He has a way to synchronize us with His speed about things that need to happen for Kingdom advance. I have already drawn heavily upon Romans 8:26-27, 1 Corinthians 14:2 (mysteries), 1 Corinthians 2:9-13 (words which the Holy Spirit teaches), John 14:26, and John 16:12-15 to make this case. I believe one of the reasons it has taken so long for the Gospel to be preached to the ends of the earth is that we are too busy about our own concerns and not synchronized with what's on *Abba*'s heart. Equally, we have been trained to analyze everything by the power of intellect, believing that the mind is our highest faculty of insight and intelligence. By contrast, the Scriptures clearly teach that the spirit of man (*pneuma*), and not the mind (*psuche*), is the part of man that really knows a man and can know God.

We have been trained to analyze everything by the power of intellect, believing that the mind is our highest faculty of insight.

The prophet Isaiah says this in a way that we would not properly interpret unless the Apostle Paul had made the application for us. Look carefully at this portion of Scripture.

> *Whom will he teach knowledge?*
> *And whom will he make to understand the message?*
> *Those just weaned from milk?*
> *Those just drawn from the breasts?*
> *For precept must be upon precept,*
> *precept upon precept,*
> *Line upon line, line upon line,*
> *Here a little, there a little.*
> *For with stammering lips and another tongue*
> *He will speak to this people.*
>
> Isaiah 28:9-10

Isaiah is painting a word picture of the darkness and deafness of the Old Testament human condition. Because life had left man's spirit due to the Fall, man could only acquire knowledge in the mind—and that through the five physical senses. He had become totally blind and deaf to the reality of a spiritual dimension. His spirit was darkened and alienated from God, so he could only process with the faculty of his mind which had access to a small portion of the data we call reality. Isaiah says, "How can man learn or truly understand?" His insight can only be "here a little and there a little, line upon line, precept upon precept." In other words, it's kindergarten learning—the way a child learns by rote memory.

Until believers take seriously what God's written revelation teaches about how we know God, hear from God, and commune with God Spirit-to-spirit, the Church and its leadership will be limited in their ability to synchronize with both the direction and speed of God's will and purpose. Amazingly, Isaiah gives an answer which is centuries ahead of his own dispensation:

> *But with stammering lips and other tongues I will speak to my people.*
>
> Isaiah 28:11

Unless Paul had quoted this passage in his instructions to the Corinthian church about the benefits of spiritual language (1 Corinthians 14:21), we would have scarcely connected these dots. By the Spirit, Paul sees that the prophet was giving his readers a preview into the New Covenant life of Spirit-indwelt, Spirit-filled believers where learning comes from the deep things of God, by the Spirit of God, directly into the spirit of man.

5. Spiritual language energizes supernatural rest and peace from the inside-out.

There is another key benefit of spiritual language we can learn from Isaiah. Let's read one verse further in the Isaiah 28 passage to glean this additional benefit:

> *For with stammering lips and another tongue*
> *He will speak to this people,*
> *To whom He said, "This is the rest with which*
> *You may cause the weary to rest,"*
> *And, "This is the refreshing;"*
> *Yet they would not hear.*
>
> Isaiah 28:11-12

Again, we can understand what the Holy Spirit was saying through Isaiah by looking at Paul's interpretation. Through spiritual language, not only can we receive knowledge from a different place, but also receive rest, strength, and refreshing from the inside-out. The following verses point to a man's spirit as the fountainhead of his strength and power:

> *Keep your heart* [Hebrew: leb—inner man] *with all diligence,*
> *for out of it spring the issues* [forces] *of life.*
>
> Proverbs 4:23

> *The human spirit can endure in sickness,*
> *but a crushed spirit who can bear?*
>
> Proverbs 18:14 (NIV)

Out of man's spirit flows the forces of life, even the strength to endure sickness and every kind of hardship.

As noted in the previous chapter, brain research has shown that the frontal lobe of the brain (where decision-making occurs) gets extremely quiet while speaking in tongues. Researchers note that "the brain is very much awake but very much at rest."[41] Wouldn't it make spiritual sense that if man is made in the image of God—an integrated three-in-one being—that the forces of life would flow out of man's spirit?

It is common knowledge that physical rest alone cannot provide the refreshing that our souls really need. Every home could tell stories of anticipated vacations and experiences that failed to provide the true renewal the soul was thirsting for. The reality is that:

> *In* [God's] *presence is fullness of joy;*
> *At* [His] *right hand are pleasures forevermore.*
>
> Psalm 16:11

Spiritual language is the *Abba Cry* of the Spirit within our spirits that brings true rest and refreshing—making His yoke easy and His burden light.

6. Spiritual language allows the Holy Spirit to strengthen you with every kind of strength you need in your inner man.

Paul tells the Corinthian church—and others who would read the letters—that spiritual language is not just about public manifestation but private edification. He says:

> *He who speaks in a tongue edifies himself,*
> *but he who prophesies edifies the church.*
>
> 1 Corinthians 14:4

In an attempt to devalue the necessity of spiritual language, some Christian leaders have asserted that here Paul is telling the Corinthians that anyone who speaks in tongues (prays out of his spirit) is just puffing up his own ego. However, if this was indeed Paul's intent, he would not have followed that statement by saying that he who prophesies edifies the church. He's certainly not saying that the church's ego is puffed up! He is speaking of both personal spiritual growth (through speaking in tongues), and the spiritual growth of the church (through prophecy). Furthermore, a few sentences later Paul expresses:

> *I thank my God I speak with tongues more than you all.*
>
> 1 Corinthians 14:18

If we look at the consistency of Paul's words to all the Church, we can see that he is saying the same thing to the Ephesian church when he prays ...

Every kind of strength you need is made available to you by the Holy Spirit through your spirit.

> ... *that He* [the Father] *would grant you, according to the riches of His glory, to be strengthened with might through His Spirit in the inner man.*
>
> Ephesians 3:16

How do we receive strength? By mental exercises? A little. By physical exercise? Paul says it profits a little (1 Tim. 4:8), but the real rest and refreshing comes by the Holy Spirit strengthening you and me in our "inner man"—the human spirit. Jude says it again using slightly different terminology:

> *But you, beloved, building yourselves up on your most holy faith, praying in the Holy Spirit...*
>
> Jude 1:20

What kind of strength do you need? Endurance, faith-receptivity, persistence, strength to forgive .... Every kind of strength you need is made available to you by the Holy Spirit through your spirit. If we don't know how to draw that out, we are no different from the poor man who inherited millions of dollars but never found out about it. Praying in the Spirit is one of the primary ways that we partner with the Holy Spirit to receive everything God has prepared for us to live lives of godliness, power and purpose.

7. Spiritual language promotes psychological wholeness and resistance to depression.

In the previous chapter I shared that one of the beautiful features of spiritual language is that it is a tangible, physical witness that God is living inside you. Allow me to draw from several sources in the fields of Psychology and Neurology (specifically brain function) to underscore this point and expand on the psychological benefit of the exercise of spiritual language.

John Kildahl, from the federally-funded research entitled "The Psychology of Speaking in Tongues," speaks of the results of the *Minnesota Multiphasic Personality Inventory*—specifically observing the impact of spiritual language on those who practice it. He says:

> The results of the MMPI revealed that *glossolalists* were characteristically less depressed than non-glossolalists. When tested a year later, the *glossolalists* continued to experience the same feelings of well-being; they were neither more nor less depressed than a year previously. They continued to say they were "changed persons" and continued to feel a definite assurance that God loved them. Furthermore, they described themselves as more sensitive and loving toward others. Many felt they had better marital, including sexual, relationships. Most reported higher moral and ethical responsiveness which they attributed to the glossolalia experience.[42]

He concludes that, "tongue-speakers have a profound sense that they are well."

D. A. Tappeiner says in the *Journal of the American Scientific Affiliation*:

> It is easy to see why tongue-speakers are less depressed than non-tongue speakers. Depression is a feeling that the cupboard of the world is bare, that good things are not possible for oneself, and that the supply of good things in the world "out there" is limited. A *glossolalist* believes that God Almighty ... is with him and approves of him, and that fellow believers surround him and confirm him in his belief that he is alright. It is hard to conceive of a more powerful antidote to feeling depressed ... Should he feel a bit down, he can begin to speak in tongues and recall that God is with him, that *glossolalia* is a special gift from God, and that he can unload his problems through releasing his feelings through tongue-speech.[43]

According to Dr. Raymond T. Brock, an ordained minister of the Assemblies of God, Professor of Psychiatry and missionary with 48 years of ministry:

> There are some of us who believe that *glossolalia* is conducive to good mental health and assists in personality integration. It is an

experience that comes to grips with pathological (illness) tendencies in fragmented personalities and offers the "better way" Christ came to impart … Speaking in tongues assists the Spirit-filled believer in achieving this wholeness and perpetuating it in everyday life.[44]

D. A. Tappeiner also sees the integrative results and says, "A truly healthy person is one whose basic experience and actions are organically rooted in the deepest impulses of life."[45] Moreover, Morton Kelsey, Episcopal rector and psychologist said, "Speaking with tongues is evidence of the Spirit of God working in the sub-conscious and bringing a person to a new wholeness, a new integration of the total psyche."[46]

The reality is, the mind was never intended to carry the load. When a person's spirit takes the lead, the soul and body will be able to function in the support roles they were designed to fulfill. Out of man's spirit flow the forces of life.

8. Spiritual language helps us locate our "spirit man."

Many Christians struggle with hearing God because they think He is speaking to their mind (thinker), but God is a spirit and generally speaks to your spirit (your knower)—the hidden man of the heart, your inner man. Notice that Paul explains,

> *If I pray in a tongue, my spirit prays.*
> 1 Corinthians 14:14

When you pray in the Spirit, your spirit is talking. Your mind wants to fight it because we have been trained to pay attention to our minds. By praying in the Spirit, you are making a declaration to your mind and body that you will only be ruled by the S/spirit, and not by your soul. This is spiritual exercise, much like strength resistance training. The more you exercise your spirit the more you locate it. Know the voice of your spirit over the voice of your mind, and you will more easily discern the voice of God. *I have yet to meet a person who prays in the Spirit regularly who has ongoing difficulty hearing the voice of God.* That's my experience.

I have yet to meet a person who prays in the Spirit regularly who has ongoing difficulty hearing the voice of God.

127

9. Spiritual language activates a spirit of faith.

Jesus was very clear in His teaching that our faith is a determining factor in the outcome of our prayers:

> *For assuredly, I say to you, whoever says to this mountain, "Be removed and be cast into the sea," and does not doubt in his heart, but believes that those things he says will be done, he will have whatever he says. Therefore I say to you, whatever things you ask when you pray, believe that you receive them, and you will have them.*
>
> Mark 11:23-24

This is disturbing to some people, because we don't want to acknowledge that we may be weak in our faith. The good news is that God himself has come alongside—by the Holy Spirit—to teach us how to live by faith. To be sure, He doesn't teach us as a lecturer who gives us information and walks off. Instead, He works from within us to activate in us a spirit of faith. Paul said:

> *Since we have the same spirit of faith …*
> *we also believe and therefore speak.*
>
> 2 Corinthians 4:13

It is no secret that the Scriptures point to the combination of what one believes in the spirit/heart and says with the mouth, as a key to spiritual power. Even entrance into the Kingdom by the new birth is initiated by "believing with the heart … saying with the mouth."

> *That if you confess with your mouth the Lord Jesus and believe in your heart that God has raised Him from the dead, you will be saved. For with the heart one believes unto righteousness, and with the mouth confession is made unto salvation.*
>
> Romans 10:9-10

Jude reinforces this principle of faith saying,

> *But you, beloved, building yourselves up on your most holy faith, praying in the Holy Spirit…*
>
> Jude 1:20

When your mind is full of doubts, you can still build up faith in your spirit. Don't miss this dynamic Spirit-and-word interaction. It is the same principle displayed in creation when the Spirit hovered over the dark void and "God said." When we pray in the Spirit, we are engaging our hearts with our mouths as the Holy Spirit forms the words in our spirits. If you demand being able to understand this supernatural operation with your natural mind, you will cheat yourself out of this benefit.

10. Spiritual language releases ministry reservoirs; rivers of revelation, communication and demonstration (power).

By "rivers of revelation, communication, and demonstration" I am referring to the manifestation of the Spirit that Paul describes in 1 Corinthians 12:8-10.[47] Jesus alluded to these rivers shortly before His crucifixion. John records:

On the last day, that great day of the feast, Jesus stood and cried out, saying, "If anyone thirsts, let him come to Me and drink. He who believes in Me, as the Scripture has said, out of his heart will flow rivers of living water."

John 7:37-38

To make sure we don't misunderstand what Jesus was talking about, John gives us a footnote:

But this He spoke concerning the Spirit, whom those believing in Him would receive; for the Holy Spirit was not yet given, because Jesus was not yet glorified.

John 7:39

John makes the connection and explains the impact of Spirit fullness in a believer's life. We don't receive the Holy Spirit for our own benefit. Jesus expects us to be so full that there will be an overflow. He describes it as rivers of living water. Where a river runs, people can see its impact. However, how much of the river of the Spirit are we seeing in our churches?

Because our Western enlightenment culture has so heavily influenced the Church, spiritual (*pneuma*) development has been subordinated to emotional and mental development in the pursuits of ministry education. We

What do you expect to happen when you go to church? have taught best practices, protocols, and psychological principles and called it ministry training. Subsequently, there is a generation in leadership on the horizon that scarcely knows the difference between anointing and personal charisma, prophecy and preaching, worship and fog machines, TED talks and teaching, or pastoring and management.

Our concern should not be whether someone gets offended because they come to church and see something they have never seen before. Our concern should be that they come to church and fail to see something they've never seen before! What do you expect to happen when you go to church?

Paul explained why he chose to minister by the demonstration of the Spirit's power rather than through the eloquence of man's wisdom. He said that if he leaned on his natural abilities to preach the Gospel, the end result would be that believers' faith would rest in what men could do, but if He ministered by the Spirit, their faith would rest on the power of God:

And my speech and my preaching were not with persuasive words
of human wisdom, but in demonstration of the Spirit and of power,
that your faith should not be in the wisdom of men
but in the power of God.
1 Corinthians 2:4-5

Remember, Paul had just come from Mars Hill in Athens, where he had used the rhetorical skills he had learned in Tarsus to speak to the philosophers. He saw a little spiritual fruit, but not much. He went down to Corinth:

Determined not to know anything among you except Jesus Christ
and Him crucified.
1 Corinthians 2:2

Paul was adamant about the importance of partnering with the Holy Spirit to see His manifestation "for the common good" (1 Cor. 12:7). Notice that Paul begins his letter to the Corinthians with a thanksgiving prayer of what they had received by the Holy Spirit:

You were enriched in everything by Him in all utterance and all
knowledge, even as the testimony of Christ was confirmed in you, so
that you come short in no gift.

1 Corinthians 1:5-7

If Paul's ultimate goal was to minimize the manifestation of the Spirit among the Corinthians, this would have been a strange way to greet them. On the contrary, he not only encourages them but also stimulates them to a better understanding of partnership with the Spirit as a way of being. Paul didn't intend for his letters to be separated into chapters and verses as we have them in our modern translations. He would have expected them to read the letter in its entirety. So, we see that he devotes ample time (in our versions 1 Corinthians 12 through 14) to talk about supernatural ministry. It is in this context that he addresses spiritual language and says:

I wish you all spoke with tongues ... I thank my God I speak
with tongues more than you all ... desire earnestly to prophesy,
and do not forbid to speak with tongues. Let all things be done
decently and in order.

1 Corinthians 14:5, 18, 39-40

There is a direct correlation between the exercise of spiritual language and the manifestation of the Spirit's gifts. We are not to choose one or the other, but practice both. When we cultivate our partnership with the Holy Spirit in private (in the Word and praying in the Spirit), we are more likely to know how to partner with Him when He wants to show God's goodness to others through us. (For a fuller treatment of this subject see my book, *The Gifts of the Spirit for a New Generation*).

Consider all the benefits available to every believer—a taste of heaven to come, made available to an orphan world that wants to see this kind of loving God. He is looking for sons who will take on the Father's unfinished business, with the Spirit's power and in the authority of the Son. If you hang out with the Holy Spirit, He'll make you look smart, powerful, courageous, loving and submitted to the will of the Father. My prayer is that you, too, will make the Holy

If you hang out with the Holy Spirit, He'll make you look smart, powerful, courageous, loving and submitted to the will of the Father.

Spirit your passion and quest; that you will refuse to live without your friend, guide, and teacher.

I want to know the Holy Spirit's voice better than any voice on this planet.

What Have We Said?

Praying in the S/spirit enables us to participate at a preconceptual (beyond our imagination) level in the conversation of the Trinity.

Spiritual language enables communication with God that bypasses the limits of your mind.

Spiritual Language enables you to pray accurately, according to God's will.

Praying in the Spirit—our spirit by the Holy Spirit—is how the Holy Spirit synchronizes our hearts to what is in the Father's heart.

Spiritual language is a primary way that God downloads His will and purposes for your life.

Praying in the S/spirit provides supernatural rest and strengthens you at the deepest place with every kind of strength you need.

Spiritual language promotes psychological wholeness and resistance to depression.

Praying in the S/spirit not only helps a person locate his/her spirit (as distinct from the soul) but releases a spirit of faith as we learn to connect our hearts with our words.

Praying in the S/spirit enriches the believer with rivers of revelation, communication, and demonstration (the nine gifts of the Spirit, 1 Cor. 12), and increases our love for others so that the gifts are used in the right way.

PRAYER

*Holy Spirit, I am asking for nothing less than for You to be my best
friend. I don't even understand how that can possibly happen, except
that Jesus said that He has sent You to be with me, to lead me, guide
me into all truth and show me things to come. That sounds like a best
friend to me. Father, I was never meant to live without the benefits
of the indwelling Holy Spirit. I'm asking You to fill me with Your
Spirit again. I yield my need to understand with my analytical mind
everything You want to do in my life. I ask You to flow through me
to bless others with rivers of revelation, communication and power.
Thank You for filling me with Your love for others and a boldness to
give that love away. In the name and realm of the Father, Son
and Holy Spirit. Amen.*

GROUP DISCUSSION

1. Of the ten benefits listed, which would be the greatest help to your walk with the Lord and to your effectiveness in helping others?

2. What testimony or story can you share that relates to your own experience with one of these benefits?

3. In what ways do we see scientific research reinforcing or informing what we understand biblically about the benefits of praying in the S/spirit?

Eight

Impacts of Sonship on Prayer

That day I learned the difference between a petitioner and a son
— Author Unknown

A director of a benevolence ministry in Great Britain had an idea that needed funding. He had the opportunity to present his project to the Duke of Edinburgh, Prince Philip, the husband of the Queen of England. Though not a king, the Duke carries out certain functions of power and authorization of the release of funds, especially in terms of benevolence. The director said, "I just knew if I could get a hearing with the Duke of Edinburgh and could present my ministry to him, then there would be provision and resource for us." So, he submitted his request to present his petition by formal letter.

In time he received a reply with the royal seal that said, "Your request for petition has been granted … such and such date, at such and such time …. You are scheduled to meet for a hearing with the Duke of Edinburgh." The letter went on to give pages of specifics; he would only have fifteen minutes, he would dress a certain way, present himself at a certain gate at the palace, at a certain time, etc.

He began to prepare, because he knew that with only fifteen minutes, every word would be important. He wrote and rewrote his petition, memorized it verbatim, and on the specified day he arrived at the right gate, at the right time, wearing the right attire. He was escorted by royal guard to the Duke, where he waited. In short order he was summoned and found himself seated in front of the Duke of Edinburgh.

The Duke politely but seriously said, "You have fifteen minutes," as he turned the quarter-hourglass over. The petitioner began the presentation that sounded like old news to him now. He was scarcely two minutes into the presentation when, all of a sudden, a side door burst open and little Prince Charles bolted through the side door crying, "Daddy, Daddy! My toy is broken!" Without even thinking, "Daddy" turned in his chair, rose, walked out the side door with his son, and spent nine minutes fixing the toy. He came back and sat down, saying, "Excuse me. I had to attend to my son. You

We have made prayer into a complicated methodology for twisting God's arm, and it doesn't need twisting.

now have four minutes." The man, with hurried, garbled speech, got his points out and was summarily dismissed.

You can imagine the frustration of the ministry director. Over the following weeks he mused repeatedly on the event. The end of the story is that the petitioner did receive financial assistance from the Royal Palace, but he came away with something better. "The greatest lesson I learned that day," he said, "is that there is a difference between a petitioner and a son."

The son can come breaking in any time (because the door is open) and say, "Daddy! Daddy!" and the Father's heart runs to meet the need. We have taken the promises of God and the invitations of our Father and turned them into a petitioning program. We have made prayer into a complicated methodology for twisting God's arm, and it doesn't need twisting. Dr. Jack Hayford has said many times over the years, "Prayer is not overcoming God's reluctance. He wants good for us more than we do." There's a stark difference between a petitioner and a son.

Sonship Transforms Our Prayer Life

It's the orphan spirit that clamors to be heard but fails to understand the difference between a petitioner and a son. Conventional wisdom says, "It's the squeaky wheel that gets the grease," but Father says, "If you would just enjoy My presence, come to know who you are as a son, and let My Spirit rise up in you, life as you know it would change forever." When that begins to happen, you begin to hear something new coming out of the depths of your heart. It is a new sense of belonging. You find your heart brimming with confidence to burst into your Father's room shouting, "Daddy! Father!" How do you do that? It's a journey, a road to walk. The Holy Spirit is at work, transforming our hearts so completely that when we feel compelled to take the shortcut we hear something come up from our spirits that says, "I have so much more for you."

There are three Greek words in the New Testament that show the growth and maturing process of sons. The first one is *paidion*. The term has an etymological connection to "pedagogue." A pedagogue is a tutor who leads, guides and teaches a child, but the pedagogue is not a member of the family. When the child grows and enters the adolescent stage, another term is more applicable: *teknon*. As *teknons*, sons are considered capable of adult activities. They can fall in love but may not have the maturity for marriage. They can drive a car, but as mentioned before, they may not have the wisdom to know when, where, or how fast to drive it. They are physically able. They may have the motor skills and intelligence, yet lack the needed emotional maturity to be entrusted with the full freedom we would give to a mature son. Then there's a third word in the Greek, *huios* (whee-os), that points to this idea of maturing sons that take their place of adulthood and can be entrusted to share in their father's business.

Again and again, the Lord calls us to a place of sonship and says the way you begin to take your place as sons is through learning obedience by the Spirit. Jesus, the Son of God, living among us as the Son of Man, learned obedience through the things He suffered (Heb. 5:8). Do you remember the boyhood story of Jesus in the temple confounding the doctors and the lawyers? Mary and Joseph start their journey home, unaware that Jesus is not in the caravan. They assume their son is with their friends and family. Once they discover he is missing and return to Jerusalem to find Him, He says, *"Don't you know that I must be about my Father's business?"* (Luke 2:49).

Then the next verse says that He subjected Himself to His parents. He went back and submitted Himself to someone who didn't have as much revelation as He had—they didn't have the insight into the Father's business that He had. This is where many of us miss it. We come to a place where we know more than our parents (or teachers, pastors, leaders) do. We see their flaws. We see their faults. We see their inadequacies and say, "I can do better than that." We refuse to submit ourselves to others simply because they don't have the revelation we have, but Jesus modeled submission (a heart attitude, not just a behavior) under those who didn't understand or know what He knew. By submitting to them, God honored Him and approved Him. Jesus modeled the difference between petitioners (someone moved by need) and sons (someone moved by obedience to the Father's voice).

Impacts of Sonship on Prayer

Why do we need to consider the impacts of sonship on our prayer-life? Because without an understanding of the divine-human partnership of prayer, and the grand scheme of spiritual authority given to us as sons, we may never open our hearts to the prospects of prayer. If we don't understand that the *Abba Cry* (partnership between God's Spirit and the believer's spirit) is one of the chief ways sons are to take their place in the drama of redemption, we may assume God has chosen to work unilaterally, or worse yet, is limited to the natural ways of man. To see the contrast between orphans (petitioners) and sons with regards to prayer, please consider these eight impacts on the prayer life of sons and daughters. As you study these truths, ask the Father to reveal any area He might want to speak to you about.

1. A spirit of sonship produces boldness and confidence to approach the Throne of Grace.

Without a spirit of sonship, we will either be too timid to come to God (fearing we don't measure up or carrying the residual shame for some past failure), or we will glibly come without the awe and fear (reverence) of God. Jesus, however, invites us to "Come boldly to the Throne of grace to obtain mercy" (Heb. 4:16). Notice how Jesus almost pleads with His disciples to "come and ask anything!" He appeals to them on the basis of a relational change. They are no longer "servants" but friends, because the servant doesn't know what the Master is doing, but the disciples have been brought into the inside information, the knowledge of the Father's mission (John 15:15).

> *This is the confidence that we have … if we ask anything*
> *according to His will … he hears us.*
>
> 1 John 5:14

Orphans will always struggle with confidence in the Father's presence until they receive a revelation that no one enters the Throne on the basis of his/her own performance.

2. A spirit of sonship provides the heart desire, a "want-to" to be with the Father.

With a spirit of sonship we come to the Father, not just to petition for our needs and wants, but for intimacy—to know and be known. I suppose no wisdom surpasses that of simply spending time with God every morning. Knowing Him and hearing His voice, in the many ways that He speaks, keeps us tuned to the *Abba* reality and a sonship consciousness. When God speaks in us, His words create the will and desire to do what He says. The power of His words create the will and desire; His words fill us with Himself. Orphans will struggle, trying to conquer temptations of the flesh by willpower to prove they are "good Christians" or "at least as worthy as the next guy." It is the Spirit, however, that creates a heart desire that precedes our desire to pray, empowering us to discover prayer as the place where the *Abba-Cry* transformation happens.

3. A spirit of sonship recalibrates a son or daughter to want to know what is on the Father's agenda.

Jesus said to His disciples:

> *No longer do I call you servants, for the servant does not know what his master is doing; but I have called you friends, for all that I have heard from my Father I have made known to you.*
>
> John 15:15

This is the heart of sonship in the Trinity; sons are brought into knowledge of the Godhead because Jesus delights to make the Father's will and purpose known to His friends. By the Holy Spirit we are calibrated to the Father's heart to restore the broken creation, which results in hearts to pray. We cannot sustain a passion for the mission (the people who need to hear the Father 's voice) without tenacious, fervent prayer for those who are living without it.

4. A spirit of sonship recalibrates our understanding of our elder brother Jesus' ongoing role as faithful High Priest.

The orphan spirit approaches prayer as an individualistic duty with the subtle mindset that "the burden is on my own shoulders to make something happen; therefore, I must pray using the right formula, saying the right words, entering the Throne Room ever so cautiously." The orphan spirit says in cunning ways that our approach to God is on the merits of good standing.

By contrast, a son knows that we only have access to the Father through the one acceptable sacrifice of Jesus and His ongoing substitutionary work

Our sonship is voice-activated by the Holy Spirit. Paul tells us that it is the Holy Spirit who activates and shapes our prayer. as High Priest. The burden is never actually on us to get things done. When we believe it is our prayer that is making it happen, we have no inkling of the holiness (transcendent otherness) of God. He allows us to participate, and we are to never discount the importance of that participation as sons. I am not saying everything is already fixed and we are only pawns being moved around on the cosmic chessboard. I am saying, however, that we are in the Throne Room because we are in Him (Jesus), not as individuals who have figured it out. Our access to God is through Jesus Christ by the Spirit.[48]

5. **Prayer is the result of the Holy Spirit's work and stirring in our hearts.**

The *Abba Cry* is not only convincing us that we are sons (John 16:8; Rom. 8:15) and calibrating us to the Father's voice (Luke 10:21-22), but it is also the energizing work of the Spirit within us, creating in us the very desire to pray! Prayer is really nothing more than getting in on the conversation of the Triune God—what the Father is saying to the Son, what the Son is saying to the Spirit—and how the Spirit and the Son are bringing our earthly condition before the Father and drawing us into that fellowship and mission. Our sonship is voice-activated by the Holy Spirit. Paul tells us that it is the Holy Spirit who activates and shapes our prayer, because we don't know how to pray as we should (Rom. 8:26-27). Can you see that you would have no desire to pray whatsoever except that the Holy Spirit is in you creating and energizing that desire (Phil. 2:13)?

6. **Sonship grants us authority to pray, and that authority includes a restored role of rulership in creation.**

We understand that a son has rights. The prodigal son had a right to his inheritance (Luke 15:11-32), but he exercised his right out of an orphan spirit. Jesus, on the other hand, demonstrated a sonship submitted to the Father's mission. He went down into the waters of baptism. He submitted to the way of righteousness and came up in the power of the Spirit. Notice that Jesus submitted to His cousin, John, in the Jordan River. He submitted to someone who didn't really understand what was coming next. John the

Baptist only knew that this was the One, the Lamb of God who takes away the sins of the world. He declared it by saying, "His shoelaces I'm not even worthy to tie." He had that much insight, but he didn't know much else, and it wouldn't be long before he would be asking, "Is this the One, or should we look for another?"

Jesus submitted Himself to the ministry of someone who knew far less than He did. We call that humility. He said, "This must be fulfilled for righteousness' sake." When He came out of the water, the heavens opened and the Father's voice was heard, "This is my beloved Son ...." From that day forward, Jesus began to draw on the resources, the inheritance, and the provision of Heaven. This was not for His benefit, to make His life comfortable or to insulate Himself from other people so that He might not get hurt again. Instead, He stewarded the resources of Heaven to break the yokes of bondage and darkness off of other people and to bring many sons to glory.

What is our sonship about? Our sonship is not admittance to the luxurious life of isolated royalty so that we can insulate ourselves from others, but so that we can bring many sons to glory. Jesus demonstrated for us that the Son has responsibilities—the responsibilities of the Father's mission and the ordered realm of the Kingdom, the responsibility to hear the Father and only do that which He sees the Father do and speak only what the Father speaks to Him.

7. Sons move in partnership—a relational rhythm of rest and dignity.

Jesus modeled sonship for us in "doing only what He saw the Father doing and saying only what He heard the Father saying" (John 5:19; 12:50). This is why Jesus never succumbed to the pressure of the crowd to perform miracles at will or to only say what would be pleasing to their ears. He healed the sick and did good in partnership with the Holy Spirit (Acts 10:38).

As I write these pages, the Winter Olympics are being beamed daily by satellite technology, and Chiqui and I will watch a couple of prerecorded highlights at night. One of the intriguing characteristics of the Winter Games is that so many of the events are team sports that depend upon being in a perfect synchronized rhythm with one's partner or team. Bobsledding, pairs figure skating, and team speed skating are examples, not only of the necessity of teamwork, but also rhythm. A number of sports involve several members of a team, each playing his/her position and doing his/her part.

141

When we are doing the ministry of Jesus, we are simply doing what we see Him do by the same power of the Spirit. But some of these sports require every member of the team to make the exact same movements at the exact same time. Did you know that you can speed skate faster as a team than you can as an individual?[49] Like geese flying in formation, the speed skaters match one another's rhythm perfectly, take turns in the lead, and draft off of the leader to increase speed and conserve strength. This is why Jesus could say "My yoke is easy and My burden is light" (Matt. 11:30). When we are doing the ministry of Jesus, He has actually taken the lead (it's His ministry), and we are simply doing what we see Him do by the same power of the Spirit. He has actually called you to draft off of Him, staying in rhythm with His every move so that we can also say, "I only do what I see Him do, and say what I hear Him say." There is also a dignity about this rhythm.

Think about Prince Charles or his sons, Prince William or Prince Harry, of the United Kingdom. As fascinated as we may be by the British royal family, we must admit that we do not know much about royalty. These men, however, were born into something that is very natural for them—a way of being that is "first nature," not second nature for them. Their wives, on the other hand, married into royalty and had to receive extensive training on protocols. In a very real sense, you and I are born into royalty by being born again, and we have also married into it as the Bride of Christ. We have to learn to live in the consciousness of who we "be." We learn by the Spirit that we don't have to push, pull, manipulate, demand, or fret, though that still feels natural to us at times.

The "relational rhythm of rest" simply means that we grow into our new reality in such a way that we can become more and more at rest in who we are. We discover that we spend less and less energy trying to defend our new identity or convince others (and ourselves) that it is really so. Dignity is living in the confidence of your real identity. The more we learn to partner with the Holy Spirit through a daily ongoing conversation of prayer and praise—the inhale and exhale of ongoing communion with God by the Spirit—the more we enter the "rest" of faith. Prayer is not trying to force God's hand, nor is it an attempt to prove we have faith or check off the boxes of our spiritual disciplines. This sonship prayer is a life of communion with the Father and responding to what He says. Therefore, the rest of faith is most clearly seen in a spirit of peace, praise, and thanksgiving.

8. Sons live and emit an infectious spirit of thanksgiving.

Thanksgiving comes from a heart that is rightly calibrated to Heaven. When you know that "all things are yours" and that you did nothing to deserve them, the natural result should be thanksgiving. A spirit of thanksgiving is born in sons and daughters who know they have a Father, they have an eternal home, and an inheritance that does not rust or fade away. Sons and daughters know that happiness is not derived from the things we possess here, but that we live with eternity in view and all our valuations and priorities are set by Heaven's economy. The most precious commodities in that economy are people. Therefore, when we say that sonship is first and foremost about finishing the Father's unfinished business, we are saying that our focus is on bringing many sons to glory. Thanksgiving starts here. Let me show you from Scripture.

Hebrews 11 reveals a raw but real tension of the Christian life lived between the "now and the not yet." Some heroes mentioned in this chapter lived in faith that produced great miracles and exploits of power, while others (very much in the same faith) were tortured or put to death. The outcome (some looking victorious and others looking like victims) is clearly not the measure of a person's faith. The fact is that whatever we "put our faith in" reveals where our highest values and priorities are. So, what is the point of Hebrews 11?

The writer to the Hebrew believers asserts that these men and women of faith were not looking for a comfortable life here; they had their eyes fixed on a heavenly city "which has foundations, whose builder and maker is God" (Heb. 11:10). They were not putting their hope in the circumstances of the day (though we all want things to go well), nor the comforts of this life (though there's no spiritual dividend for discomfort). They were living with a heart of thanksgiving because of the reality of what they could not see with their natural eyes.

When our eyes are on the Father and we are committed to the Father's business, we can live in a spirit of praise and thanksgiving. If, God forbid, we find ourselves in shackles in an inner prison at midnight, we can join Paul and Silas in a rowdy chorus of praise and thanksgiving, because comfort was never the goal (Acts 16:25-28). How could they praise God in such pitiful circumstances? They

These men and women of faith were not looking for a comfortable life here; they had their eyes fixed on a heavenly city.

What I am describing to you is the stark difference between sons and orphans when it comes to prayer. were on the Father's business and their objective was to bring many sons to glory. Spiritual logic would say that if we are walking with God (and we are), and we find ourselves in this jail for the sake of His name, He must be up to something! Let's give Him thanks for it before we see it! What I am describing to you is the stark difference between sons and orphans when it comes to prayer. Here's Heaven's logic:

The Spiritual Logic of Thanksgiving

- Sons of God know the Father is always up to something, so we can give Him thanks in advance as though it has already happened.

> *Rejoice always, pray without ceasing, in everything give thanks; for this is the will of God in Christ Jesus for you.*
> Thessalonians 5:16-18

- Sons don't wait for something good to happen to give the Lord thanks. The biblical pattern of the Temple is not that we leave the Temple with thanksgiving, but that we enter with thanksgiving. Thanksgiving is first.

> *I will enter His gates with thanksgiving ....*
> Psalm 100:4

- Sons can live in thanksgiving because they know the Father hears them. Our standing before God is in the Son. Jesus is standing at Lazarus' tomb while Lazarus is still dead and begins to give thanks:

> *Father, I thank you that You always hear Me*
> John 11:41

Paul and Silas don't wait for the answer before they offer up thanksgiving:

> *But at midnight Paul and Silas were praying and singing hymns to God, and the prisoners were listening to them.*
> Acts 16:25

- When sons and daughters stand before the Father with the incontrovertible authority and promise of the Son as the "Yes and Amen" to all the promises of God, it's only logical to give thanks before, during, and after whatever adversity you might be facing.

> *If you ask anything in My name, I will do it.*
>
> John 14:14

> *Therefore by Him let us continually offer the sacrifice of praise to God, that is, the fruit of our lips, giving thanks to His name.*
>
> Hebrews 13:15

- If I am to believe I receive the answers to my prayers when I pray them, the next logical thing to do is to give thanks!

> *Therefore I say to you, whatever things you ask when you pray, believe that you receive them, and you will have them.*
>
> Mark 11:24

Orphan Prayer vs Sonship Prayer

Let's consider briefly the contrasts between the impacts of an orphan spirit in prayer and a spirit of sonship in prayer:

Orphan's Prayer	Son's Prayer
The orphan spirit understands God as holy and powerful but not personally loving, so prayer doesn't look that inviting.	Sons know they are welcome, have a father, and want His presence more than answers.
A "petitioner" is asking for something that benefits him.	A Son is free to be in the Father's presence because he is a son.

145

Orphan's Prayer	Son's Prayer
Orphans see prayer as a way to get their share of the inheritance now, so prayer is often focused on receiving answers to daily problems such as money, jobs, food and clothing (Luke 15).	Sons know the Father knows what they need so they don't take thought for these things (Matt. 6:32-33).
Orphans see prayer as a duty to perform, a way to be accepted, to be "good," or possibly even prove or leverage their righteousness.	Sons see prayer as an opportunity to hear the Father's voice and discover the Father's heart.
Orphans may focus on the techniques of prayer as a cause-and-effect way to get God to act.	Sons think of prayer as conversation, discovering, abiding, knowing, and being known.
Orphans tend to do all the talking in prayer.	Sons learn that the art of honorable conversation is both talking and listening, including prayer.
Orphan prayers tend to focus on the "what," "why" and "when"— to satisfy the mind's need to know and to get the answer now.	Sonship prayers tend to focus on the who—who is God, who am I in God, who is on God's heart.
Orphan prayer can be sprinkled with blame, criticism, and information we think God doesn't know yet about a person or situation.	Sonship prayer rests in not only the Father's knowledge of all things, but also His forever commitment to every person's best and highest good.
Orphan prayer may even pray against people or leaders who seem to be the opposition.	Sons pray as though all are sons, speaking blessing and forgiveness, especially on those who curse and abuse the righteous.
Orphans pray judgment on people.	Sons pray mercy, blessing, and God's grace on people.
Orphans may tend to pray out of a busy mind and soul (emotions).	Sons and daughters pray from their spirit, as the place where the Spirit of Adoption dwells.

Prayer is not just a cry of desperation, nor is it just a running grocery list of requests. Prayer is the activity inspired by the Spirit—the Spirit in our spirits crying "*Abba*, Father"—imparting divinely inspired prayers in the hearts and mouths of believers who will partner with God as sons in the Father's business. No one demonstrated this better, or enriched the Church's prayer life more, than the Apostle Paul. No one, other than the Lord himself, gave more Spirit-inspired prayers to the Church as godly theology, modeling of intimacy, or Heaven's strategy, than Paul. What might we learn about the impacts of sonship on prayer from the man who alone gives us this "*Abba Cry*" revelation?

Before Paul was a missionary or a theologian, he was an intercessor. Before he was an intercessor, he was a son.

The Apostle Paul on Prayer

Before Paul was a missionary or a theologian, he was an intercessor. Before he was an intercessor, he was a son. This means that we could learn a lot by studying Paul's life of prayer, and thanks to his prayer-filled letters, we can learn from the prayers themselves (though our focus doesn't allow for an in-depth look).

• Notice how Paul's relationship with his churches and converts was sustained and nurtured in intercessory prayer—Paul praying for them and the church praying for him.

> *I do not cease to give thanks for you, making mention of you in my prayers ... For this reason I bow my knees to the Father of our Lord Jesus Christ, from whom the whole family in heaven and earth is named, that He would grant you...*
> Ephesians 1:16; 3:14-16

• Paul understood that there were certain aspects of spiritual development that could only happen as a result of prayer. Prayer was necessary so that a spirit of sonship (i.e., "Christ formed in you") would break through in the believers.

My little children, for whom I labor in birth [travail] again until
Christ is formed in you.

Galatians 4:19

- It was more than form and style for him to write this way. He lived prayer for the people to whom God had sent him.

Therefore watch, and remember that for three years I did not cease to
warn everyone night and day with tears.

Acts 20:31

- Paul understood that the very foundations of spiritual maturity and a sonship consciousness don't come primarily through church attendance or lots of teaching (though these are important), but in a place of prayer that partners with the Spirit's *Abba Cry* in the heart of the believer.

For as many as are led by the Spirit of God, these are sons of God. For
you did not receive the spirit of bondage again to fear,
but you received the Spirit of adoption by whom we cry out,
"Abba, Father." The Spirit Himself bears witness with our spirits
that we are children of God, and if children, then heirs—heirs of God
and joint heirs with Christ, if indeed we suffer with Him,
that we may also be glorified together.

Romans 8:14-17

But when the fullness of the time had come, God sent forth His Son,
born of a woman, born under the law, to redeem those who were
under the law, that we might receive the adoption as sons.
And because you are sons, God has sent forth the Spirit of
His Son into your hearts, crying out, "Abba, Father!"
Therefore you are no longer a slave but a son, and if a son,
then an heir of God through Christ.

Galatians 4:4-7

- Paul's prayer life was transformed by the coming of the Spirit. He saw prayer as a partnership between the believer's spirit and the Holy Spirit, commanding them:

Pray in the Spirit at all times for all the saints.

Ephesians 6:18

- Prayer in the Spirit was normal for Paul. He saw it neither as uncontrollable ecstasy nor passive surrogacy, but as partnership between his spirit and the Holy Spirit which facilitated ongoing dialogue with the Father and the Lord Jesus.

I thank my God I speak in tongues more than you all.

1 Corinthians 14:18

- Paul believed that sons and daughters aren't left to figure out how to pray; the Holy Spirit who lives within us is ever ready to help us pray both beyond the limits of our understanding and according to the will of God. We can trust Spirit-formed prayer because the Spirit knows the mind of the Lord and the depths of the Father's plans and purposes. To pray in the Spirit is to pray according to the will of God.

Likewise the Spirit also helps in our weaknesses. For we do not know what we should pray for as we ought, but the Spirit Himself makes intercession for us with groanings which cannot be uttered. Now He who searches the hearts knows what the mind of the Spirit is, because He makes intercession for the saints according to the will of God.

Romans 8:26-27

- As sons and daughters are busy about the Father's business, they can expect that this kind of ongoing partnership in prayer is the precursor to the Father's "making all things work for their good" and the advancement of the Kingdom. It should also be noted that without this kind of partnership in prayer, there is no blanket promise that covers "all things."

And we know that all things work together for good to those who love God, to those who are the called according to His purpose.

Romans 8:28

- Praying from my spirit by the Holy Spirit (spiritual language) is not speaking to men but to God, and in that communication are embedded "divine secrets." Therefore, according to Paul, this is the most effective, strategic, and accurate way to pray.[50]

For he who speaks in a tongue does not speak to men but to God, for no one understands him; however, in the spirit he speaks mysteries. ... He who speaks in a tongue edifies himself, but he who prophesies edifies the church.

1 Corinthians 14:2, 4

• Praying in the Spirit is also God's provision for His people in spiritual warfare—the ongoing struggle against the principalities and power. Gordon Fee says, "Paul urges believers to engage the enemy by the 'S/spirit weapons'—all of the armor of God is put on—suited up—by praying in the Spirit."[51] This means that the Spirit provides a way to partner with believers (with minimal risk) to penetrate the enemy's territory and rescue people who have been taken captive.

And take the helmet of salvation, and the sword of the Spirit, which is the word of God; praying always with all prayer and supplication in the Spirit, being watchful to this end with all perseverance and supplication for all the saints.

Ephesians 6:17-18

We could take several more pages to look at how Paul learned to listen in prayer as well. As a son, he lived in a clear conscience and loved the Father's presence. He received an abundance of revelations, had the Lord appear to him in visions, and received clear instructions repeatedly about his missionary journeys and specific details of his mission. Whatever else this life as a son meant for Paul, it certainly meant a life devoted to prayer, an ongoing *Abba Cry* accompanied by joy and thanksgiving because sons walk in the assurance that the Spirit is constantly recalculating our paths to the middle of the Father's will and purpose.

What Have We Said?

Prayer is a two-way conversation. It is not making demands upon God but listening, partnering, and asking, "Father, what do You want me to ask You for?" Jesus teaches us to ask the Father.

We have made prayer into a complicated methodology for twisting God's arm, and it doesn't need twisting. Prayer is not overcoming God's reluctance. He wants good for us more than we do. There's a stark difference between a petitioner and a son.

A spirit of sonship transforms our desire to pray, makes us bold to enter the Father's presence without shame or timidity, and synchronizes us with the Father's agenda.

The Holy Spirit helps us find and sustain a relational rhythm of rest that makes prayer a communion of intimacy rather than drudgery or duty. The results of this relational rhythm of rest is an overflowing fullness of thanksgiving and joy.

We highlighted the contrasts between the way orphans and sons approach prayer and saw that Paul understood an unbreakable bond between the Spirit's role in prayer and our own revelation of sonship, specifically by the *Abba Cry*.

PRAYER

Father, I am so grateful that You give me the invitation to come boldly before You to obtain mercy and find grace in the time of need. You never resist my appeals and petitions for help. I also thank You that You are inviting me to come as a son/daughter, not just because I have a need, but because I have a loving Father who already knows what I need and has already made provision. Gracious Father, forgive me when I run in and out of Your presence with appeals for help but fail to simply enjoy time with You. Would You speak to me in the next few hours, over the next few days, about the power and privilege of sonship prayer? Would You reveal to me the relational rhythm of resting in You, knowing You, knowing that I already am where I need to be, with nothing to achieve or prove? Would You reveal to me the power of ministry in the Throne Room? I start right now as one whose life emits a constant overflow of thanksgiving. May my thanksgiving be infectious, attractive to orphans who need to know You, and attractive to the atmosphere of Heaven. Thank You for making me Your very own. Amen.

GROUP DISCUSSION

1. After seeing Paul's emphasis on prayer as a key means for spiritual maturity, what questions does this raise?

2. What are some of the reasons that believers don't pray? To what degree does that tendency get transformed if believers grasp their sonship?

3. Which of the contrasts between orphans' and sons' prayer spoke to you most clearly? Why?

4. What did you sense the Lord saying to you about your own current experience in prayer?

Nine

On Mission with the Triune God

And I have declared to them Your name, and will declare it, that the love with which You loved Me may be in them, and I in them.

– Jesus

I believe the Father's desire of redemption, the global plan and purpose of redemption in the Father's heart, is to give you a home. He wants His children to be at home, to be carefree, to run, to play, and to dream. He wants His children to jump up on His lap so-to-speak and enjoy His overflowing, limitless love. In short, the mission of the Trinity is to draw mankind up into the very other-centered, overflowing life of love that the Father, Son, and Holy Spirit themselves enjoy. As Jesus prayed it:

> *... that they all may be one, as You, Father, are in Me, and I in You;*
> *that they also may be one in Us,*
> *that the world may believe that You sent Me.*

John 17:21

Many of us don't live there but under the lies of the enemy. Many believers have a new identity—the authority to function as sons in the Kingdom—but are living under a former influence. We could call it "DUI of the flesh."

DUI of the Flesh

Here's a metaphor that may help us. Let's make the connection between the natural and the spiritual. In 2012, almost 30 million Americans admitted to driving under the influence of alcohol or some other drug.[52] That is 10% of the U.S. population, which we would assume are licensed to drive. Because they are under the influence, they are operating vehicles while not thinking clearly about who they are or where they are going. The reason those statistics are tracked is that driving under the influence

The Father first gives to us anything He wishes to receive from us. is a primary cause for accidents and tragic deaths. We could say that many believers, who have been given a new identity in Christ and are baptized in the Spirit, are "driving under the influence" of orphan thinking. What kind of needless harm could this spiritual DUI be causing? While it would be difficult to quantify, we do know all creation groans, waiting for the sons of God to take their place (Rom. 8:19).

Too many believers live with the prevailing mindset that says, "You're not there yet. You don't have what it takes. You're not good enough. You have to earn it." All the while the Father is saying, "There is nothing you can do to deserve My glory. I have chosen to share it with you. Anything I ask of you, I first give to you" (John 3:27, pharaphrase). To live into this reality and get on mission with God, we must receive a revelation of our sonship. Let me say it another way, the Father first gives to us anything He wishes to receive from us. Ultimately, if God's strategy was just to get you to Heaven there would be little need for all this talk of the *Abba Cry*, personal transformation, and prayer. The mission of God is about setting you free so He can get you to join the global adventure for humanity!

The Missionary Trinity

We must understand that the mission of God is not about getting more people to think and believe the way we do, as if it were a cosmic game of "red rover, red rover, let Johnny come over." Getting more people on "our side" than "their side" is not the mission. It's about the nature of the Father as other-centered, infinite love. He is not willing that any should perish (2 Pet. 3:9). As David Bosch says, "Mission has its origin in the heart of God. God is a fountain of sending love. This is the deepest source of mission."[53] David Seamands talks about "the impulse of Trinitarian ministry" as the natural outflow of the Triune God himself.[54] Mission is not something God does, but who He is, and therefore, it's not something we are asked to do, it is who we are in the God who is other-centered and sending.

If, as we have attempted to establish in *The Abba Foundation*, the nature of the Triune God establishes everything God has made in oneness—mutual indwelling—then we must understand that the picture Jesus was revealing by the parable of the prodigal son was not so much about the son as it was the Father. Jesus paints a picture of His *Abba*, whose very nature is not just to stand and look. He is not a distant observer waiting to see if we can get ourselves out of our mess. He is the Father who runs toward His creation. This being true, it tells us much about the kind of sons God is restoring to Himself. The missional God raises missional sons and daughters.

Jürgen Moltmann suggests that the mission of the sending Father, Son, and Spirit is not entirely completed upon the death and resurrection of Jesus. Through the coming of the Spirit, His history becomes the Church's gospel for the world. The Church participates in His mission because the Church is one with the sending Trinity, but it takes an overflow of the Spirit in and through the Church for the incarnational, empowering, transformational life of the Vine to bear fruit through the branches.[55] This clarity of oneness—the connection of the source of life to and through everything else—is the ground of a proper understanding of mission as the nature of God, and the Church as the image of God in the earth.

I was raised in mission-minded churches that lived with an understanding that because "God so loved the world," He would send us out to reach that world. (Paul reframes it as a debt to the whole world in Romans 1). Nevertheless, I didn't hear my pastors and teachers in those early years framing mission in the overflowing, ecstatic, self-emptying nature of the Trinity, though it could not be any other way.[56] I had never read or heard of Karl Barth's reverse whirlpool concept, describing everything as centered in the core reality of God's three-ness relationship and flowing out of that source.

Mission is more than a doctrine of the Church to get everyone saved. It is more than an empathic desire to help men avoid a burning hell, more than an empirical strategy for global conquest, and certainly more than an ego-driven need for numerical growth. Mission is rooted in the very essence of who God is—the going-out, sending-out nature of our overflowing God who sends His Son, who in turn then sends the Spirit. Biblically it looks like this:

1. The Father sends the Son.

> *For God so loved the world that He gave His only begotten Son, that whoever believes in Him should not perish but have everlasting life.*
> John 3:16

2. The Father and Son send the Holy Spirit.

But when the Helper comes, whom I shall send to you
from the Father, the Spirit of truth who proceeds from the Father,
He will testify of Me.

John 15:26

Behold, I send the Promise of My Father upon you; but tarry in the
city of Jerusalem until you are endued with power from on high.

Luke 24:49

3. The Father, Son, and Holy Spirit send the Church.

And Jesus came and spoke to them, saying, "All authority has been
given to Me in heaven and on earth. Go therefore and make disciples
of all the nations, baptizing them in the name of the Father and of
the Son and of the Holy Spirit, teaching them to observe all things
that I have commanded you."

Matthew 28:18-20

As You sent Me into the world, I also have sent them into the world.

John 17:18

But you shall receive power when the Holy Spirit has come upon you;
and you shall be witnesses to Me in Jerusalem, and in all Judea
and Samaria, and to the end of the earth.

Acts 1:8

To say this in a slightly different way, the Father is the first missionary who goes out from Himself by creating the universe. The Son is the second missionary by going out from Heaven to save the fallen world. The Holy Spirit is the third missionary who draws mankind to purpose and empowers the Church. The Church is the fourth missionary going into all the world to bring orphans to realized sonship. Jonathan Edwards called this "a disposition to abundant self-communication."[57]

A Son Is Given

Isn't it interesting that when the Father wanted to demonstrate His love to a planet of orphans He didn't send a great leader, a great teacher, strategist, or prophet (even though we know Jesus was all of that). Isaiah reveals God's solution for the orphan planet was to send a Son:

For unto us a Child is born,
*Unto us **a Son is given**;*
And the government will be upon His shoulder.
And His name will be called
Wonderful, Counselor, Mighty God,
Everlasting Father, Prince of Peace.
Of the increase of His government and peace
There will be no end,
Upon the throne of David and over His kingdom,
To order it and establish it with judgment and justice
From that time forward, even forever.
The zeal of the Lord of hosts will perform this.

Isaiah 9:6-7

Unto us a Son is given.

Mark Hanby says:

With a lack of fathers comes a lack of identity. We need so desperately to have boundaries to know who we are. An orphan will spend his life tracing his roots, seeking any information the he can find concerning his heritage, for without a family line he will never know himself. He may have many brothers and sisters, but without a knowledge of his father, he will never be able to recognize their kinship. Perhaps he is the rightful heir to a large inheritance, but without the proof of his lineage he'll never be able to receive it. Many in Christendom today, when questioned, can point to many teachers who have influenced their lives, but cannot point to a father in the ministry. Thus, like the Corinthian church, we have abundant teaching, we come behind in no gift, but we have not many fathers. And as a result, we are gathered under the banner of organization, or doctrine, or denomination, or gifting, but have lost the sense of father-to-son relationship, through which character-based ministry is imparted. And we wonder why great leaders continue to falter under pressure. Relational patterns of ministry must be rediscovered to raise up real sons in the faith.[58]

What we have produced in the Church, especially in North America, is something of a counterpart to the world's system. If you have the gifting, the talent, the charisma, or the money, you can be somebody. It's a meritocracy (merit-based system) in which one's value is based on performance. Rather than rearing up sons, we've cultivated protégés—those who want what we have. "I want to preach like him." "I want to sing like her." "I want to be able to run an organization like him." What we don't have are sons and daughters who know how to submit to others and lift others up because their value and identity have already been established. What we must see is that restoring orphans to their sonship is not a special project on God's "to do" list. He is not about measuring performance because He has nothing to prove; neither is He measuring sons' performance as if their value was dependent on their productivity. When God revealed Himself as the "I Am," He forever established that "being" comes before "doing." "I Am that I Am" also establishes that sons, made in the Father's image, are who they are because they are sons, not because they can perform.

The Father's Mission

The Father's mission is much more than just getting everybody to think right or to provide everyone with a ticket to Heaven. Jesus wasn't sent to the earth to make a new religion. Because God is, by nature, a Father, Jesus was sent to the earth to reconcile orphans to their Father. Jesus was sent as the elder brother, telling all other sons and daughters, "Hey! Dad's arms are open wide! It's time to come home! Quit running from Father; run to Father."

All of Jesus' parables are designed to reveal the nature and heart of the Father. Therefore, once we read His parables through the Father lens, everything changes. For example, the story of the Prodigal Son is not about the son who for a season couldn't care less about his father; it's all about the heart of the father. Watch the father as he is looking out over the horizon for his son to come home. How many weeks or months did the father stand on the highest point of his property watching, waiting, and straining his eyes to see if his wayward son was returning? As soon as the father sees him, he runs to him, falls on his neck, and kisses him! At the same time the son has an orphan script playing in his head saying, "I'll just be your servant. I am not worthy." The father interrupts the prepared but pitiful speech and says, "No way! No way! Bring the robe, bring the ring, and kill the fattened calf. We're going to have a party—a sonship party."

In the same way, the cross is God the Father shouting in visible form, "No way! No way! I will not let My sons and daughters grovel with the pigs. That was never the plan. They must know that they are My sons and they will always have a home as far as I am concerned!"

Our mission is to invite people to the party of the Father's presence. It is to invite sons and daughters to the party where Father is actively healing our hurts, changing the way we see ourselves, and pouring His grace to heal our brokenness. Jesus wants us to hear the Father saying, "My son, who was lost, now is found!" If you've been home so long that "lost" seems foreign, then hear the Father saying:

> *Son, you are always with me, and all that I have is yours. It was right that we should make merry and be glad, for your brother was dead and is alive again, and was lost and is found.*
> Luke 15:31-32

Jesus' Mission

Jesus' mission was to finish the unfinished business of His Father. He said:

> *I have glorified You on the earth. I have finished the work which You have given Me to do ... I have manifested Your name to the men whom You have given Me out of the world. They were Yours, You gave them to Me, and they have kept Your word.*
> John 17:4, 6

In Father's house there are no tears, no pain, no anxiety, no sense of inferiority, and no sense of competition. Jesus has come to bring us back to Father's house. He said:

I will not leave you orphans; I will come to you.

John 14:18

In other words, He says, "I'm going to give you the Spirit of sonship so you can know your identity and inheritance, so you can know that everything you need has been provided. How do I get that to you? I'm going to come to you by the Holy Spirit." That means that after His resurrection, He is still carrying out the work and will of the Father.

Ray S. Anderson says that Christ's continuing ministry after His resurrection and ascension is a threefold apostolic ministry—all of which, of course, flows from His nature. First, His continues to be an INCARNATIONAL ministry, which means that the Church will assume forms and methods that are relevant to contemporary social and cultural forms, challenging them and renewing them while creatively using them to touch people's lives. Second, His dynamic apostolic ministry is EMPOWERING, as a continuation of His earthly ministry, directly challenging the principalities and powers of the air that hold people captive. This is underscored by Paul when he says:

For our gospel did not come to you in word only, but also in power, and in the Holy Spirit and in much assurance.

1 Thessalonians 1:5

Finally, His continuing ministry is TRANSFORMING, as the Lord of Glory, now enthroned, finishes what He started through His Church. This means that the Church will penetrate and seek the blessing and renewal of human structures relationally, that seek to de-humanize persons and discount creation.[59] The way Jesus finishes the Father's work is as important as what He is doing. Jesus is the perfectly obedient Son whose eyes are fixed upon the Father.

A Father-Focused Mission

Don't miss the theme of the Last Supper (John 13-17). The real focus of the Upper Room discourse (often called the Last Supper) is often lost in the surrounding dramas of the identity of the betrayer, of who will sit at Jesus' right hand, or where Jesus is going and how the disciples will find

Him. What is often missed is Jesus' riveted focus on revealing to His disciples that the objective is oneness with His Father. In John's account, Jesus refers to His Father 47 times in those four chapters! Here is a man that knows this is His last meal with His closest friends before His death. These are His last words to them before His death. He is almost breathless saying, "Guys, it is all about a restored relationship to the Father. I am going to prepare a place for you with My Father. We are going to none other than the Father's bosom. This is why I came!" (John 14).

Jesus served out of a consciousness of His sonship.

John begins his account of this scene by declaring that Jesus served out of a consciousness of His sonship. He knew where He had come from (the Father), knew He had all authority (from the Father), and knew where He was going (to the Father). With this knowledge—and because of this certainty—He took a bowl of water and towel and washed the disciples' feet (John 13:3-5). Following this, Jesus introduces the Holy Spirit, another just like Him, who will come, take the things of the Father and reveal them to His followers (John 14:16-18; 26-27). At the end of this chapter John records Jesus saying, "Arise, let us be going," but He can't leave. He keeps talking about His Father! "My Father is the vinedresser and I am the vine" (John 15:1). By chapter 17, after more detail on how the Holy Spirit is going to bring His disciples into the same mutual indwelling Jesus shares with His Father, He just turns His face toward heaven and starts talking to His Father directly:

> *Father, the same way You and I are one—I am in You and You are in Me—Abba, show them that You are making them one with us in the same way... and that the same way You love Me, You love them ....*
> John 17:21-23 (my paraphrase)

As I read these words, I'm overwhelmed to see that Jesus is not at all concerned with being a great leader. He's not the least bit concerned about being received as a great mentor. His objective is not to be a great man of prayer, orator, or even the founder of some new movement. After three and one-half years of powerful, miraculous ministry, one might think Jesus would be rehearsing His

One might think Jesus would be rehearsing His best miracles, His most astounding sayings, or recalling the largest crowds.

best miracles, His most astounding sayings, or recalling the largest crowds. Instead, Jesus is all about teaching His disciples about what it is to be in the Father's presence. When we read these chapters, we realize that Jesus' priority, not only here in these last hours but for His entire earthly journey, is about one thing. His focus is to please His Father—as the totally trusting Son—and to make His Father known.

In this discourse Jesus refers to "Father" 47 times. This is in just one conversation. That's a singular focus. In fact, the Gospel writers refer to the Father over 200 times and Paul refers to the Father over 150 times in his letters. It is a key, because they are older; they have experienced the Father. They know what fatherhood is all about, and know that it's a priority. We don't think about it much. Our minds are locked into being great leaders and achievers, leaving a legacy, building a brand, or being good stewards. It's not that those things are not important, but Jesus says, "It's not all about that! It's not all about performance. That's orphan thinking."

Jesus did not come to establish a new religion. Jesus did not come to create Christianity. Jesus didn't even come primarily to get us to Heaven. Jesus came to reconnect us to the Father and so fulfill the mission of love. Jesus came to rescue orphans from the orphanage and take us back to Father's house. He said:

Don't worry about your failure. I know where that's coming from…
But I am the way, the truth and the life.
No one can come to the Father except by Me.

John 14:3-6 (paraphrase)

That's the point.

We see from Hebrews 2 that the Father's mission is to bring many sons to glory:

For it was fitting for Him [the Father], *for whom are all things and by whom are all things, in bringing many sons to glory, to make the captain of their salvation* [Jesus] *perfect through sufferings.*

Hebrews 2:10

Further, we see that Jesus' mission is to open the way to reconnect sons to the Father's heart. We've turned it into a terribly difficult enterprise, but the language of sonship is a language of love. In this new kingdom, restored relationships trump everything else.

We have talked about the Father's mission and about Jesus' mission. Now we must turn our attention to the Spirit's mission. In Jesus' last discourse, in the midst of the all-consuming conversation about the Father, Jesus announces the coming of the Spirit and speaks of His mission.

The Spirit's Mission

Those familiar with the upper room discourse just before the betrayal (John 14-17), understand the importance of Jesus' announcement. He said He must go away for the Holy Spirit to come. Jesus made a direct statement about the Spirit's mission. Part of that mission is to those who do not yet believe, and part of that mission is to the believer. He said:

> *And when He has come, He will convict the world of sin, and of righteousness, and of judgment: of sin, because they do not believe in Me; of righteousness, because I go to My Father and you see Me no more; of judgment, because the ruler of this world is judged.*
>
> John 16:8-11

The Holy Spirit is not confined to working in the Church among believers. In fact, the Holy Spirit is working ahead of the Church to prepare the soil for the time when the message of the Good News arrives.[60] The Spirit is convicting and convincing the world of sin, righteousness (right-standing) and judgment. There are three aspects of His mission:

1. The world needs to know that they are suffering from sin—a broken relationship with God—and that all the brokenness of the world comes from that separation from God.

2. The Spirit is on a mission to communicate righteousness to the world—that right-standing with God is not only possible but secured by the sacrifice of Jesus. The ministry of reconciliation declares that God is not holding up or counting against men their trespasses but cancelling them (2 Cor. 5:18-21).

3. The Spirit is convicting the world that judgment is about to be rendered through the crucifixion, and with it the judgment of the great deceiver himself (John 12:30-33). In other words, now is the time to switch allegiances.

The Holy Spirit has a mission that is uniquely outside the Church, to the world. In addition, the Holy Spirit has a ministry inside the Church, to the believer.

I still have many things to say to you, but you cannot bear them now. However, when He, the Spirit of truth, has come, He will guide you into all truth; for He will not speak on His own authority, but whatever He hears He will speak; and He will tell you things to come. He will glorify Me, for He will take of what is Mine and declare it to you.

John 16:12-14

The Holy Spirit is convincing and convicting the believer about the truth of the Good News generally, but also specifically that adoption of sons is personally applied and what it means to share in Christ's own inheritance. This *Abba Cry*, which Jesus teaches Paul by revelation, replaces the many lies each of us believe about ourselves, teaches us who we are, and reminds us of what we have now that we are in Christ.

Because the Spirit of God is coming to us from the future, not the past, He will show us things to come. Having the "last days Spirit" living within each believer, it is not strange that we should know some things before they happen—that we should have insights into what is yet to come. The prophetic nature of the Church is a result of the indwelling Holy Spirit who has come from the future to take us there, totally whole, renewed and restored. Jesus teaches us to pray, "Thy kingdom come ... in earth as it is in heaven," and the Spirit is here moving us to that future end.

The indwelling Holy Spirit has come from the future to take us there, totally whole, renewed and restored.

Finally, the Holy Spirit empowers the sons of God to do the same works Jesus did, via the "gifts of the Spirit" (1 Cor. 12:8-10), which are God's supernatural endowments made available to every son and daughter of God to do the same works.

(For details about the purpose and operation of the gifts of the Spirit, I recommend my book, *The Gifts of the Spirit for a New Generation*.)

The Hearing Ear

It is important for us to notice that the key to all of this Holy Spirit teaching, guiding, convicting and convincing is the Spirit's hearing and then our hearing. Jesus says:

> *When He, the Spirit of truth, has come, He will guide you into all truth; for He will not speak on His own authority, but whatever He hears He will speak; and He will tell you things to come. He will glorify Me, for He will take of what is Mine and declare it to you.*
> John 16:13-14

Did you catch that? How does this *Abba Cry* work? The Holy Spirit is listening, listening, listening. We infer from Paul's understanding that the Holy Spirit lives in the Triune communion, where Father and Son are talking about their good purpose and plans for you and me. The Holy Spirit "searches out the deep things of God" and then comes back to reveal those things to you. He listens, then "He will tell you what is to come" (1 Cor. 2:10-12).

To get the full picture we need to put three passages together: John 16:5-16, 1 Corinthians 2:10-15, and Revelation 5:1-10. In John 16 Jesus tells us *what* is happening. In 1 Corinthians 2:10-15, Paul describes *how* it happens. Finally, in Revelation 5:1-10 John takes us into to the Throne Room scene to reveal the *when* and *where* it is happening.

John sees Jesus in the Throne Room, taking a scroll, opening it, and reading from it. What is He reading? The scroll represents the Father's last will and testament for each one of us. In other words, Jesus is reading the unfolding of all of God's redemptive plan for the earth and humanity. He is reading the "deep things of God" about each one of us. This includes the Father's purpose for you. Jesus, as executor of the Father's will, not only dies—which puts the will into effect (Heb. 9:15-17)—but also serves as the attorney who reads the will to the family, apportioning the inheritance!

In other words, when the Holy Spirit is creating and releasing the *Abba Cry* in you, He is taking those things that Jesus received from the

A revelation of your sonship has the greatest impact upon your life, and the greatest single discipline you can learn is to hear the Father's voice. Father and passed on to Him and is now revealing those things to your spirit. This is happening simultaneously both in the Throne Room of heaven and in your spirit right now. This means that the Holy Spirit's hearing is very important, and your ability to hear is very important. If you don't hear what the Holy Spirit is saying in your spirit, you miss out on what Jesus is giving you from the Father! Henri Nouwen says:

> It is the Spirit of God showing us continually how to move from opaqueness to transparency; that is, it clears away the illusions and helps us see things as they really are, which opens us to transcend just the thing and see new possibilities far beyond the person or situation itself.[61]

Here is the cure to your problems. This is the shortest distance between two points, the fastest way to get from where you are to where God is calling you to be. *You must cultivate your inner ear to hear the Father's voice.* Cultivate habits that put you in a place to hear His voice. Learn to quieten your mind, get in His presence, pray in the Spirit, and listen.

Jack Hayford often says, "You can't cast out the flesh, and you can't disciple a demon." Sometimes we have the right tools but don't know where to use them. An orphan spirit cannot be cast out, prayed out, or counseled out. The orphan spirit cannot be psycho-solved. The orphan spirit is only conquered by a revelation of the Father's love, and that comes by hearing His voice. The orphan spirit is displaced by the revelation that you are a son or daughter of God. Jesus came to show us the Father (John 14:9), and He gave us the Holy Spirit to fill us from the inside out with the knowledge of His will and spiritual understanding. A Spirit has given to us that cries within us "*Abba,* Father." This being the case, a revelation of your sonship has the greatest impact upon your life, and the greatest single discipline you can learn is to hear the Father's voice.

Opposition to His Sonship

Jesus lived His life in the awareness of the Father's love and the Father's mission. He spoke as a Son sent from a far country to plant His father's vineyard (Matt. 21:33-39). The religious orphans hated Him and tried to kill Him. Don't mistake it. It's an orphan spirit that senses sonship and tries to snuff it out. The enemy's plan is to keep you in the limitations of Lodebar, the wasteland where orphans live, where everyone is doing the best they can and trying to validate their significance and worth.

Have you wondered what it was that angered the Pharisees most about Jesus? He claimed sonship of the Father. Among all the false charges thrown at Jesus at His mock trial, the only compelling accusation He would not deny, was about Him being the Son of God (Matt. 26:62-66). More than anything else, the Pharisees were afraid of losing their position and power. They said:

> *If we let Him* [Jesus] *alone like this, everyone will believe in Him,*
> *and the Romans will come and take away both our place and nation.*
> John 11:48

That is the orphan spirit at work. It's the spirit that lives in fear of losing position and power, assuming those are the source of personal identity.

Why do you suppose you have not heard that much about Jesus' focus on bringing you into a revelation of your sonship? Why have you not heard more about Jesus' last night with His disciples being all about showing them the Father (John 14:7-10)? Why do you suppose much of the Church focuses on right behavior, ethical and moral codes, and being a "good Christian" rather than listening to the Father's voice as sons and daughters? Could it be because Satan wants the Church to remain in the bondage of an orphan spirit? The good news is that Jesus said in that same last meal:

> *I will not leave you orphans; I will come to you …*
> *But the Helper, the Holy Spirit, whom the Father will send*
> *in My name, He will teach you all things, and bring to your*
> *remembrance all things that I said to you.*
> John 14:18, 26

The *Abba Cry* that the Holy Spirit is forming in your heart right now is calling you from the meager living of the orphan spirit to a life and language of love. This is the life of other-centered, free self-giving in the Father's mission. Once you realize you really are a son of the Father who has

There is no greater adventure than giving yourself away, knowing God will see to it that you have all you need to make Him known. it all and can make more if need be, you can freely give yourself away. You will never lack again. There is no greater adventure than giving yourself away, knowing God will see to it that you have all you need to make Him known.

In the next chapter we will consider why this transformation is important and how God empowers us with gifts of the Spirit to supernaturally connect us with people who are not aware of the Father's love. Walking as sons is the most exciting life in the world.

What Have We Said

God has given us His Spirit, not just to get us to Heaven, but to get us on His mission for humanity.

We have talked about the Father's mission to redeem mankind and all of creation.

The Son's mission is both to finish the Father's unfinished business and to make His name known.

We talked about the Spirit's mission to reveal the ways of Father and Son to us by convicting, convincing, teaching and guiding us into all truth.

The Spirit calibrates us to an understanding of what Father, Son, and Spirit are up to in filling the earth with the knowledge of the Lord. He knows how to connect us supernaturally with people.

PRAYER

Abba, I come to You, offering nothing but myself, as a little child, depending totally upon You as my source for everything. Abba, I feel Your love for me. There is nothing better than being loved by You and knowing that I can put Your kingdom first and live on mission with You without fear of what I will eat or what I will wear. You are freeing me from bondage and fear by the indwelling Holy Spirit, so I can be about Your business. Because I am being filled with Your Spirit, I have joy in accomplishing the mission that You have impregnated in my heart. Thank You, Holy Spirit, for dreams, visions, passions, and kingdom pursuits that are being birthed in my spirit. This is no legal-load carrying mission. You are teaching me where I came from, where I am going, and my authority in You, so I can freely serve. I am not trying to get somewhere or be somebody. I am open to receive Your love and give it to others. Father, I am making myself available to be on mission with You. Amen.

Group Discussion

1. Explain what we mean by "the Missionary God."

2. How does this chapter reveal the Father as a missionary? What is His mission?

3. How does this chapter reveal the Son as a missionary to the world? What is His mission?

4. How has the Holy Spirit been sent into the world? What is the Spirit doing on mission?

5. What does this mean for us as sons of God?

Ten

The Purpose of Transformation

I will remember the works of the Lord;
Surely I will remember Your wonders of old.
I will also meditate on all Your work,
And talk of Your deeds.

– Asaph

We have not been called to share the Gospel to fulfill some religious duty, but for the people we meet to hear the good news that Jesus loves them, died for them, and has made a way for them to be reconciled to God. We don't heal the sick because "it's what we do;" we heal the sick to relieve people of their pain and suffering, and to please the heart of a Father who wants wholeness for all His creation. We don't cast out demons to exercise and display our authority; we cast out demons because we love the person and want to see him free from torment and bondage. We haven't been granted the power to raise the dead so we can have a "raising-the-dead" story, but we raise the dead to give mothers back to their sons, sons back to their fathers, and husbands back to their wives. We do it to give people their lives back with a hope of eternity with God. This is where it becomes relatively easy to see the difference between orphans and sons.

All we have studied in this *Abba* series about your freedom and transformation is never intended to be an end in itself, though the Father delights to see every believer come to live and walk in his/her sonship. Your transformation becomes a glorious conduit through which others can receive healing and freedom! God empowers you to comfort others with the same comfort with which He comforted you (2 Cor. 1:4), and by it He shares His glory with you.

There are many reasons believers fail to see the freedom of others as the purpose for our own transformation. One of those reasons is that orphans misinterpret power as a badge of identity rather than the means to share the loving compassion of the Father. Sonship is about identity. We don't lay hands on the sick, cast out devils, or work miracles because

Sons don't prophesy so people can be impressed by their spirituality. we need to prove who we are. Instead, we live in the revelation that our identity is not secured by anything we do but by what He has done for us. On the other hand, many believers won't even risk ministering God's compassion in power, and then look with some disdain on those who at least make the effort. Frankly, I would rather be with folks that do their best to give God's love away, even if they are trying to fill their own deficiencies in the process. God knows how to turn up the volume on the "*Abba Cry*" in the hungry, willing heart.

Sons don't prophesy so people can be impressed by their spirituality. Sons prophesy to reveal the heart of God to the person receiving the prophecy, thus conveying the deep love of the Father. We do the works and ministry of Jesus for the Father to receive the inheritance He has chosen, the full reward for the suffering of His Son. This is the joy set before Him. Doing the stuff of ministry is never about hitting ministry goals, fulfilling religious duties, or garnering bragging rights. It has always been about loving each person and seeing each one reconciled to a loving Father. It includes destroying the works of the devil until he is finally and forever vanquished.

Let's note again that the Gospel writers repeatedly underscored that the motivation of Jesus' power encounters was not to prove something about Jesus, but to serve as the conduit of the Father's overflowing love as compassion:

> *But when He saw the multitudes, He was moved with compassion*
> *for them, because they were weary and scattered, like sheep having no*
> *shepherd.*
> Matthew 9:36

> *And when Jesus went out He saw a great multitude; and He was*
> *moved with compassion for them, and healed their sick.*
> Matthew 14:14

> *Then Jesus, moved with compassion, stretched out His hand and*
> *touched him, and said to him, "I am willing; be cleansed."*
> Mark 1:41

Ultimately, Jesus didn't heal the sick and do miracles to prove He was God. He had nothing to prove. As Paul records it:

> [Jesus], *though he was in the form of God, did not count equality with God a thing to be grasped.*
>
> Philippians 2:6 (ESV)

He healed and delivered because He was moved with compassion. By compassion, we mean that overflowing love in the heart of the Father who takes off running toward His prodigal as soon as He sees him on the horizon (Luke 15).

We do the ministry of Jesus because we are both moved with the compassion that moves Jesus, and anointed with the same Spirit that anointed Him.[62] Do you need more of that compassion for others? We'll wait for you if you'd like to stop right now and say, "Father, I have a zeal to do Your work, but I'm not sure if it's because I really love people. Would You fill me with your compassion for others? Would You give me eyes to see people the way You see them?" Amen.

Telling Our Stories

It is always a bit dangerous to tell one's own story—especially spiritual stories. People can assume you are trying to set yourself up as the guru. Others *will* set you up in their own minds and make the mistake of measuring themselves against your own experience. And, of course, there is the inherent subjectivity—seeing the story only through the narrow lens of self. Children are often good observers but poor interpreters, and I concede that I am not always a good interpreter of the things I have experienced. However, while acknowledging the possible landmines, we cannot deny that the most powerful tool the Holy Spirit has to communicate transformation from one person to another is by telling the story.

Russell Crowe won an Oscar for Best Actor in the movie "Gladiator" (2000). When asked for his comments backstage he simply said, "The narrative, the narrative. God bless the narrative." The narrative is the story, and it is a powerful weapon.

Don't be afraid to tell your transformation stories. The spirit of prophecy is the testimony of what Jesus has done in your own life (Rev.

19:10). When you tell what God has done, the Holy Spirit is present upon your words to repeat that transformation work in someone else. When a person gives glory to God by telling a story of being healed physically, for example, the "power is present to heal" again, faith is created in the hearts of the hearers, and the Holy Spirit moves toward faith.

I was awakened this morning with personal memories running through my head—memories of childhood experiences with the Holy Spirit. "Get up and write," the Spirit said. I can only assume there is something in my story that another generation needs to hear, possibly so something will be awakened.

Childhood

I saw myself as an eleven-year old boy praying back in "the prayer room" of my childhood church. I grew up in a praying church. Our habit was to arrive at church as much as an hour before service, along with countless others who joined regularly for prayer. Men would pray on one side of the room and women on the other. The room was usually kept fairly dark. It was a way to be "alone with God" even in a room full of people. It was not unusual for tears to flow, commitments to be made, full surrender to be articulated, "Lord, I will go wherever You want me to go, do whatever You want me to do."

I cannot count how many times I would reemerge from that place with God, return to the auditorium where all the folks would be gathering for service, and the presence of the Lord would come upon me, speak to me in songs, hymns, and spiritual songs. I was called to the ministry in that dark prayer room at that early age. It would be years of learning to walk with the Holy Spirit before fully discovering what the Lord had planned for me.

Then I saw another scene—another memory of me as a boy, praying. It was at a Royal Ranger Pow Wow (my childhood denomination's version of a Boy Scouts camp out, but with spiritual purpose). One of the men had spoken to us that night and, as usual, we were invited to come to the altar and respond to what the Lord was saying to us through the message. That night I knelt at a rough pine wood altar and poured my heart out to God. I don't remember the message now, nor even why I was so moved, but I remember that I got lost in the Father's embrace. I remember tears flowing on my face (along with everything else that requires a lot of tissues). I had poured my heart out to God and time meant nothing. When I got up from that place the world was clean, my soul was clean, and my heart was full. I didn't know how long I had been there alone, and I didn't care. My older soul now longs for those deep cleansing streams again and again.

Adolescence

I remember a much smaller prayer room in the church we attended during my teenage years. It was always brighter and, because of its lack of space, the compressed proximity to everyone else meant that it never had that "alone with God" feel to it. Nevertheless, I recall many Friday nights in that prayer room, gathering with our small youth group to pray before going out to "witness." I remember my first experiences of prophesying in that little prayer room. I remember seeing my teenage friends "turned into another man" as the Spirit of God would come upon them and they would prophesy things beyond their knowledge or comprehension. I was baptized in the Spirit in that same church, and supposing that building is still standing, could take you to the spot where I met God.

I remember prayer meetings at Bible College and then into my early years of ministry as a youth pastor. My closest friend, Paul Anderson, was a powerful intercessor—he would join me on Saturday afternoons or early Sunday mornings, in the prayer room, and we would "call down heaven," encourage each other with strong prophetic pictures and probably slightly outlandish admonitions to take the Gospel to the whole world. Those prayer meetings marked my soul.

Adulthood

Then I remember a troubling time. I was in my late twenties and pastoring my first church. I had hit a real rough spot in my marriage. Yes, I was still praying, and now gathering intercessors and leading prayer meetings and movements, and nonetheless having trouble in my marriage (life doesn't just go perfectly because we pray). My praying grandmother happened to be at my parents' house about an hour away and I knew she would pray for me. When I arrived, Grandma was sitting on the couch in the living room.

After a few brief greetings I said, "Grandma, I need you to pray for me." She immediately began to pray in the Spirit. As was her habit, she started praying for missionaries and pastors. She prayed "around the world" so to speak. I knelt down in front of her, took her hands and put them on my

God usually wants to talk to us more about who we are than whatever problem or pressure we may be facing.

head and said, "Grandma, I need you to pray for *me!*" She kept praying fervently, and mostly in the Spirit.

There's something you should know about my grandmother. She had learned to pray by necessity because she was married to an alcoholic and abusive oilfield worker. Grandma stayed with him (contrary to the counsel of many) and prayed fervently and continually for his salvation. He finally surrendered his life to Christ at the age of 73. Grandma knew how to pray!

I'm not sure if she ever prayed specifically for me that day, but while I was kneeling there the Holy Spirit said, "The mantle I placed upon your grandmother for prayer, I now place upon you."

Two things seemed strange to me in that moment. It was not that Grandma never really seemed to get around to praying specifically for me—I was quite sure the Holy Spirit was taking care of that through her praying in the Spirit (Rom. 8:26-27). What seemed strange was, first, "Why would God skip a generation, passing the mantle to me while skipping my parents?" I have a better understanding now that spiritual generations and natural generations are not always the same thing. The second was, "Why is God talking to me about a calling in prayer, when clearly what I need is help in my marriage?" It opens another subject altogether, another book for another time, but God usually wants to talk to us more about who we are than whatever problem or pressure we may be facing in a particular moment. It is not that He is lacking empathy for any of our feelings, but this relational God knows that wholeness is found first in our being. I'm usually asking "what," "when," and "why" questions while Father is wanting to talk about the "who"—who He is and who I am in Him.

As I write these words I am filled with gratitude for these stories and dozens more—a heritage in prayer and in the Spirit that I realize is not everyone's story. For me this is neither a point of personal pride nor a sense of exclusivity, but a humbling sense of calling that I will spend my life leaning into. So, let me ask you, what are your stories? Where are the altars you have built in your progressive encounters with God?

Last night, as I was driving home from church, the Holy Spirit came again, as though something was stirred deeply within me during the worship time at church that had not yet been fully released. I prayed with what we used to call "a strong unction," a forceful inner compulsion to pray fervently. It was a DUI experience—definitely "driving under the influence," but not in a bad or dangerous way. This is what the Holy Spirit dropped in my spirit during that encounter: *"The gifts of the Spirit are free, but not automatically passed down from generation to generation. You must be intentional to apprehend it for yourself and keep fanning the flame."* Allow me to explain.

The gifts of the Spirit are free, but not automatically passed down from generation to generation. You must be intentional.

Every morning, when I wake up, there seems to be a veil, like a membrane, separating the spiritual and physical dimension. I have to be intentional to poke a hole in that membrane and reach into the other side to lay hold of what God has for me (and others) for that day. I don't understand why all the reaching I did yesterday doesn't result in an ongoing "breezeway" in the Spirit. Perhaps for some, it does. For me, however, every morning I endeavor to be intentional about pressing through the veil of this flesh and my inability to see at will into the spiritual realm. I start each morning with a song of praise, lifted hands, prayer, and thanksgiving. It's not often that my flesh just can't wait to praise God. I have to be intentional to consciously connect to God by the indwelling S/spirit on a daily basis.

How about you? Do you ever feel that it's just easier to go along to get along? Do you feel that life is just easier if we stay busy doing the natural tasks that need to be done and ignore the spiritual dimension? Yes, it may be easier on the flesh and emotions, but I know this: the whole earth is groaning, waiting for the manifestation of the sons of God (Rom. 8:19). Someone has to pick up the torch and start praying as if the next generation won't get it unless we do. Someone has to prevail in prayer and praise until this next generation gets hungry for God and begins to have experiences for themselves in the Spirit. Someone has to be gripped with the reality that the glory of God isn't passed to the next generation automatically. Each generation must be birthed in the things of the Spirit and the things of the Spirit birthed in them.

The life of the Spirit—partnering with the Holy Spirit and making room for the *Abba Cry*—makes everything else seem trivial once it comes. Until it comes, however, we must contend for it. I pray that you and yours would experience the same kind of breakthroughs in your life.

Learning to Walk as Sons

The disciples had similar experiences with Jesus in prayer. At one point it became so apparent that Jesus was in a different league than anything they had ever heard, they pointedly asked, "Lord teach us to pray." He taught them, introducing God to them in a new way:

> *When you pray, pray like this,*
> *"Abba in heaven, hallowed be your name."*
> Matthew 6:9

Another significant prayer experience happened the night Jesus was betrayed. This is found in John 13 through 17. This portion shows us Jesus teaching His disciples, first in the "last supper" upper room setting and then on the Mount of Olives, where we witness the most intense personal prayer we can imagine just before He is betrayed. We are not told how long this dinner and prayer meeting lasted, but we do know they would begin the preparation for supper just before sundown and that it was customary to take several hours to partake of the meal. It was a very relaxed affair. As you can imagine, these being some of Jesus' last words before His death, that He would be sharing and rehearsing to them the issues of greatest importance. Therefore, from these chapters we can glean the core concepts of how we are to walk as sons.

Sons Take Constant Advantage of Direct Access to the Father

If we were to read through this setting (John 13 through 17), as though sitting at the table with the disciples, some things would stand out.

First, the Lord repeats again and again, even five times, that there's going to be immediate and direct access to the Father. Jesus says,

> *And in that day you will ask Me nothing. Most assuredly, I say to*
> *you, whatever you ask the Father in My name He will give you.*
> John 16:23

There will not be an intermediary. You won't have to go to Jesus and have Jesus go to the Father for you. You can ask the Father directly. Three other times He says, "Whatever you ask, I will do." Jesus is telling His disciples that a huge change is about to take place. Never before had humanity known this freedom of direct access to God. Even if you consider Adam and Eve in the Garden, we must note that God comes to them on their turf, so to speak. But now, we are ushered into the very throne of God.

Through Jesus Christ man has direct access to God and can know God personally.

To grasp the larger literary picture, this is the bomb the Apostle John is dropping on the world with his Gospel account: through Jesus Christ man has direct access to God and can know God personally. This was unimaginable news which we largely take for granted now.

Orphans hide from God because they have believed lies about His disposition. They have believed He reaps where He does not sow, He is a hard task master, brutal, unfair, and full of trickery. This hiding brings about relational distance that exacerbates the problem because the further one is removed from the light the more darkness, deception, and distortion finds its home in the orphan heart. *Abba*, however, comes to the orphan and dispels the lies. Note these significant invitations.

*I will not leave you orphans; **I will come to you.***
John 14:18

He who has My commandments and keeps [tereōs—cherishes, nurtures] *them, it is he who loves Me. And he who loves Me will be loved by My Father, and **I will love him and manifest Myself to him.***
John 14:21

*If anyone loves Me, he will keep My word; and My Father will love him, and **We will come to him and make Our home with him.***
John 14:23[63]

God says, "I will come to you. I will manifest myself to you. We will make Our home in you." Notice that Jesus is announcing to these disciples, just hours before it all seems to fall apart, that He and the Father are going to be coming to them and manifesting themselves to them (by the Holy Spirit). This is direct access. We are transformed, not from a distance, but face-to-face.

But we all, with unveiled face, beholding as in a mirror the glory of the Lord, are being transformed into the same image from glory to glory, just as by the Spirit of the Lord.

2 Corinthians 3:18

Sonship happens in the presence of the Lord, and we only walk as sons by learning to live in and contend for the presence of God.

If you have been waiting for the "six steps" to walking in sonship, this is as close as it will get. The first step is to learn to live in, cultivate, and practice the presence of God. How many ways can we do that? When you fall in love with that special someone, do you need a list to figure out how to spend time with them? Probably not. You will find a way to be with him/her, even if it means staying up into the middle of the night. Nevertheless, allow me to offer some suggestions from personal experience.

Cultivate a Place to Meet God

Even if you are the kind of person that hates routine, you need to develop that discipline of giving "the first" to God. You may go through seasons where it is not as consistent as you would like. It's not about performance or proving something. It has little to do with your salvation, but it has a lot to do with your "first love" and staying full of the Spirit.

Cultivate a Time to Meet God

David said, "Early will I seek you" (Ps. 63:1), but he also worshipped at the various watches of the day. Your work or school schedule might dictate the time, but remember, you'll never conquer much if you can't conquer your own physical appetites. Possess your vessel in sanctification and honor (1 Thess. 4:4)

Cultivate a Way to Meet God

The best way is whatever way puts you in the best place to most consistently hear His voice and experience His presence, but you may want to try new things occasionally to keep your time with God fresh and creative. May I suggest a few key encounter triggers?

<u>Worship the Lord with music.</u> There are many tools now to create an atmosphere of worship (mainly through songs), but the danger is that you find yourself surfing the net, posting on social media and texting, instead of focusing on the Lord. Consider worship music on some format other than your smart phone. Find music that is more vertical (conversation between you and God) than horizontal (talking to others about God). Vertical worship employs first- and second-person language (I, we, you, us). Horizontal worship tends to use third-person language (he, him, they, them). Sing *to* the Lord instead of *about* the Lord as much as possible. Pour your heart out to Him, bless Him, give thanks to Him. Make declarations as to who He is, whether you feel like it or not. Most importantly, don't let someone else do your singing for you. Worship God by lifting your own voice. He loves hearing you.

<u>Worship the Lord with the Scriptures.</u> Develop ways to read from various parts of the Scriptures daily. I have used the One Year® Bible for almost thirty years. I don't fret if I miss a day here or there because I know I will come back around to that same passage next year. That way, if the Lord leads me to focus on one passage for a season, it's not a worry. You can also use a myriad of topical tools or declaration and meditation pages to build yourself up in particular areas.

<u>Worship the Lord with physical expression.</u> Lifting your hands, bowing down, standing, dancing, and shouting to God are not "Charismatic things." All of those are biblical expressions, found mostly in the Old Testament. In fact, you will find that the English word "praise" (as in "Praise the Lord") is used to translate ten different Hebrew words behind it that may mean sing, clap, play an instrument, lift your hands, bow down, shout, emit a high sound, spin and dance, and sing unpremeditated songs. There is something very powerful about getting your physical body engaged in worship that opens you to the presence of God.

<u>Be ready to write what you hear.</u> If you were going to listen to a business guru or a personal coach you would take something to write with and something to write on. Consider your daily appointment with God at least as important and never go to God without some way to write down what you hear. You want to cherish, watch over, carefully attend to the words He speaks to you. In fact, it may be that your expectation to hear from Him could have something to do with whether or not you do. A good resource for developing a good daily hearing and writing practice

The ministry of the Spirit is so important that it is essential that a priority be given to an internal work. is Wayne Cordeiro's *The Divine Mentor*.[64] One of the most powerful results of writing what you hear in your times with the Lord is that you can go back later and see how the Lord brought you through your journey or remind yourself of prophetic words the Lord gave you. You can even use your journal as a source for writing when you are ready to pass on to others what the Lord has done in you.

<u>Go boldly and frequently to God.</u> Beyond a daily time, direct access means going boldly to God any time. For some who have developed a daily time, place and way to meet God, this can settle into a routine. We think about God during that 30 minute "appointment" and forget about communing with God until tomorrow, same time and place. As we have said, however, the key to sonship is Spirit-fullness, not fake fullness or routine. The key is living and walking in the Spirit all day, every day.

Sons Understand the Daily Importance of Communion, Fellowship, and Spirit Fullness

You have probably seen the sign posted in the dentist office that says, "You don't have to floss all your teeth, only the ones you want to keep." Daily brushing and flossing points to the importance of keeping the germs out for oral health. Jesus tells His disciples that the ministry of the Spirit is so important that it is essential that a priority be given to an internal work. Notice that in this most critical hour, when Jesus is about to be turned over to the authorities like a common criminal, He talks about direct access to the Father and introduces the indwelling Holy Spirit.

> *I tell you the truth. It is to your advantage that I go away; for if I do not go away, the Helper will not come to you; but if I depart, I will send Him to you ... When He, the Spirit of truth, has come, He will guide you into all truth; for He will not speak on His own authority, but whatever He hears He will speak; and He will tell you things to come. He will glorify Me, for He will take of what is Mine and declare it to you. All things that the Father has are Mine. Therefore I said that He will take of Mine and declare it to you.*
> John 16:7, 13-15

Think about this: The Holy Spirit gives us everything that Jesus has. What does Jesus have? Jesus says, "All the things the Father has are Mine." That sounds like the inheritance of a son, doesn't it? He's talking sonship language. He is talking about what a son knows when he lives in the perfect love of a perfect Father. "All the things the Father has are Mine, and the Holy Spirit will take of Mine, and will declare it to you." Quite simply, the most direct line, the shortest distance between the two points—from living as an orphan to living as a son—comes down to this interaction: learning to live in relationship with the indwelling Holy Spirit.

What's important is not wearing a label that says, "I've got the Holy Spirit." The indwelling Holy Spirit enables us to walk as sons and daughters, receiving what Jesus had—a spirit of sonship. With a spirit of sonship comes intimacy with the Father, a spiritual home, and the certainty of an inheritance.

In *The Abba Factor* we explained that an orphan spirit carries with it fear, bondage, isolation, deception, and control. By contrast, a spirit of sonship has everything that's antithetical to that: relaxation, peace, fearlessness (perfect love casts out all fear), an atmosphere and the oxygen of love, and knowledge that whatever Father says, He will do. In the orphan spirit there is no confidence that tomorrow is taken care of, but in the spirit of sonship, there's no worry about tomorrow, because "Everything the Father has is mine." The son is not even pressured by time, so tomorrow is no burden to him. Remember Jesus said:

> *Seek first the Kingdom of God and His righteousness*
> [keeping your spiritual relationships right], *and all these things will*
> *come to you as a matter of course.*
> Matthew 6:33, (Ben Campbell Johnson paraphrase)

When you put that in sonship language, it says that when you are mature enough and able to handle the Father's business, He gives you the Father's business along with the Father's resources. One of those chief resources is to employ spiritual language.

Spiritual Language is how God brings heaven to earth.

The Holy Spirit prays through us in a language our minds doesn't understand, and by that Spirit-to-spirit communication we receive "divine

Sons are anointed with the same Spirit, to do the same works, out of the same motivation of love and compassion as Jesus did.

mysteries," the plans and purposes of God for us and others. Paul says:

> *For he who speaks in a tongue does not speak to men but to God, for no one understands him; however, in the spirit he speaks mysteries.*
>
> 1 Corinthians 14:2

Other translations say "secret things" or "hidden things," but this word (Greek: *musterion*) refers to those things which were at one time secret, but now are revealed, as Paul describes in 1 Corinthians 2:10, 13 (see chapter 1).

I am not saying that believers cannot know and experience sonship without being baptized in the Holy Spirit. Neither am I saying that it is impossible to experience sonship without a regular practice of praying in the Spirit. I am saying that the New Testament is clear that this benefit is available to every believer (Acts 2:38-39) and that it is a primary way that God has freely given us to accelerate our spiritual growth and carry out His mission. We discussed this in detail in chapters 5 through 8.

Sons Understand That We Are to Continue the Ministry of Jesus

If this "Lord's Supper" conversation (John 13-17) shows us anything, it is that Jesus fully intended the disciples to carry on His ministry by the same anointing of the same Holy Spirit with which He ministered. He said:

> *Most assuredly, I say to you, he who believes in Me, the works that I do he will do also; and greater works than these he will do, because I go to My Father. And whatever you ask in My name, that I will do, that the Father may be glorified in the Son. If you ask anything in My name, I will do it.*
>
> John 14:12-14

These are shocking statements, but they are unmistakably clear. Sons are anointed with the same Spirit, to do the same works, out of the same motivation of love and compassion as Jesus did. There is no mincing of words. Jesus says, "it is essential that I go away so the Holy Spirit will come."

With the Spirit's coming, the ministry of Jesus gets multiplied all over the world. Luke's second treatise, the Acts of the Apostles, is written to verify that this is exactly what happened. The Holy Spirit was poured out, the Church received Him, they were all filled with the Spirit (Acts 2:1-4), and they went everywhere doing the same miracles and works Jesus had done.

Orphan's Works or Son's Works?

History tells us that, in too many occasions to recite, we heard the message about doing the same works of Jesus but missed the motivation. We didn't wait until we were moved with compassion, filled with the Father's love by the Holy Spirit. We responded as orphans trying to prove they have the sons' anointing. However, we really can't love each other with an orphan heart. Orphans don't have the capacity to really love because they haven't been able to receive love. The orphan spirit says, "I can't afford to love you because I may not get any love back, so I have to love myself, and myself only, protect myself, prove myself, and provide for myself." Nevertheless, the longer you live in close relationship with the Holy Spirit, the more the fears fall away. We learn both to receive love and to give love. We learn (sometimes so slowly) that the Father is ready to give to us as we give healing, life, encouragement, miracles, and provision away to others. The Father loves you, and there is nothing in Him but love. For many of us it takes a lifetime to see that it is not in the receiving, but in the giving, that we walk as sons.

The Ultimate Purpose of Our Transformation Is to Connect People to God

Jesus was saturated in His Father's love. He knew where He came from and where He was going, so He was free to serve. Notice how John sets up the scene of Jesus' washing His disciples' feet:

*Jesus, knowing that the Father had given all things into His hands, and
that He had come from God and was going to God, rose from supper
and laid aside His garments, took a towel and girded Himself. After
that, He poured water into a basin and began to wash the disciples' feet,
and to wipe them with the towel with which He was girded.*
John 13:3-5

If you know that Father's love is going to take care of you no matter what happens, you can afford to be treated or mistreated any number of ways without that being a threat to your identity. To be fully transformed means the fear is gone. It means living out of a revelation that the overflow of the Father's love fills you so that you can love anybody and everybody. You can love the lovable and the unlovable because your identity is not dependent upon how others treat you. Your identity is anchored in who you are in the *Abba* of Jesus.

Sons carry the Father's business in their hearts to bring the orphans back to the Father's table. By the Spirit's transformation our personal objectives begin to change. We become sensitized to people's brokenness, woundedness, sickness. We become aware that we carry the answer. We learn to look into people's eyes and quietly ask the Father, "*Abba*, how do You see this person? What do You want to do in this person's life? What do You want to say to this one?"

Todd White was one of the most broken individuals imaginable before he met Christ.[65] He was (by his own admission) such a scoundrel, that when you hear him tell his story you might be tempted to dislike him. God, however, met him, changed him, and began to teach him about his sonship. Todd was so transformed by this encounter that he wanted to give this new love away. He says that he prayed for 900 different people to be healed (not in church but in the streets, store, bars, and coffee shops) before one person ever got healed. Since then, however, he started seeing ten to thirty people healed every day, most of them in bars where he was delivering ice. Todd just wanted to connect people to God. He learned he was a son, how to stay full of the Spirit, and to keep his focus on the Father's unfinished business.

I don't have to compare my stories to Todd's. I'm not Todd, but my "playlist" of stories is growing. Baristas at Starbucks, waiters and waitresses at restaurants, people in the hospital, on airplanes, and neighbors, all need the Father's love. I continue learning how to look into their eyes and ask the Father, "How do You see them Father? What do You want to do for them? What do You want to say to them?"

Iris was a young waitress that came to our table shortly after we were seated in a Tex-Mex restaurant in North Dallas. She introduced herself and handed us menus. When she brought our water and took our order my wife said, "By the way, it's our habit to pray over our food before we eat, and we would like to pray for you too. Is there anything that you need God to do for you?" Her response shocked us. She recoiled, said, "Why would you ask me that?" and walked away briskly. I thought, "Uh oh, this might be one of those sensitive individuals who might accuse us of a 'micro-aggression'." We saw her walk to the kitchen and begin talking with another waitress. The manager came by our table to ask if everything was OK. We replied affirmatively.

A few minutes later, Iris came back to our table and apologized. She explained, "I'm sorry I reacted that way. It's just that I've been sick all day—so sick that the manager told me to either get my act together or go home. So I went into the restroom and just said, 'God if You're there, can You please do something?'" Then, she said, "I came out of the restroom, came over to wait on you, and when you said, 'Can we pray for you?' I almost lost it. God sent you to me. I didn't know how to react and that's why I ran off."

Needless to say, we prayed for Iris (she actually reached out both hands to take hold of ours), commanded the sickness to leave (in a normal tone of voice), blessed her and said, "Amen." As we were eating our food, the manager came walking by very slowly, and said, "May I ask what you did to Iris?" We explained that we had just offered to pray for her. He said, "Well, she has been sick all day. But right now she is on the phone telling her mom that she has been healed and feels perfectly well." Then he came a little closer and whispered, "What does it feel like to be able to do something like that?" We were able to give the love of the Father to him as well.

In the next chapter we will look at how the gifts of the Spirit are available to sons and daughters who are out to finish the Father's unfinished business. The presence and gifts of the Spirit are free and readily available, but they are not automatically passed down from generation to generation. God has called you to partner with the Holy Spirit to see that the knowledge of the glory of the Lord covers the whole earth like the waters cover the sea, but you have to be intentional about it. This is why the Holy Spirit is tenaciously transforming us from orphans to sons.

What We Have Said?

The gifts of the Spirit are free, but not automatically passed down from generation to generation. We must be intentional to apprehend the things of God for ourselves and for others.

In Jesus' discourse (recorded in John 13-17) we see that sons are bold to take advantage of their direct access to the Father. The Father and Son come to us by the presence of the Holy Spirit. Our responsibility is to make room for His Presence by cultivating a time, a place, and a way to meet with God.

Sons understand both the importance of staying full of the Spirit daily and the role that spiritual language can play in that ongoing fullness.

Sons understand that we are to continue the ministry of Jesus—the same works, and greater works, by the same Spirit—of healing and wholeness, and connecting people to the Father.

PRAYER

Abba, Father, how can I express my gratitude that You have given me direct access, just like this prayer, to come boldly to You by the name and authority of Jesus? How can I articulate rightful thanksgiving that You would not only save me, but make me whole enough to partner with You to bring orphans back to Your house? Thank You for filling me with Your Spirit again and again until I cannot keep Your love to myself. Fill me again with Your Spirit now, I pray, and teach me to see people through Your eyes. Teach me to ask in the moment, "Father, how do you see them? What do You want to say to them?" Teach me ways that are natural for me to be intentional about breaking through the apparent membrane that separates the spiritual and the natural. I ask You, precious Father, to touch my generation with Your glory. Amen.

GROUP DISCUSSION

Look at John 13-17 and see how Jesus teaches His disciples that they will have direct access to the Father after the Spirit comes.

1. What are some ways listed that we can "cultivate" access to the Father?

2. How does Jesus teach His disciples in John 14 and 16 that staying filled with the Spirit is of daily importance?

3. What does Jesus say in John 14 about our participation in His ongoing ministry?

4. Think about (and share) one of your own stories of how you have connected others to God.

Eleven

You Say You Want a Revolution

You say you want a revolution, well, you know
We all want to change the world
You tell me that it's evolution, Well, you know
We all want to change the world.
— John Lennon and Paul McCartney

If you have walked the full journey of this three-part *Abba* series, you have encountered the importance of a right view of God. In *The Abba Foundation* we sought to connect the dots between where our views of God come from and how that view—whether He is perceived as judge, law-giver, enforcer, goodie-giver—determines how we see everything else. We have looked through the lens of Jesus to see God as first and foremost the relational Trinity of other-centered, overflowing love who created the universe, not out of necessity but as overflowing love.

In *The Abba Factor* we examined how the original orphan, Satan, lied about the goodness of God and distorted a very good world into an orphan planet, and how God immediately set out to restore that orphaned humanity back to sonship. We contrasted the mindset of orphans and sons, articulating the progression of the orphan spirit and the progression of a sonship mentality. We sought to bring awareness to the reader of the telltale signs of orphan thinking so we could invite the Holy Spirit to do the work in those interior places where we have believed lies about God and ourselves.

In this volume, we have taken you to the interior work of the Spirit, who "searches out the deep things of God" (His plans and purpose for us) and how He deposits those plans and purposes into our spirits using spiritual words and spiritual language. The goal has been to bring you, dear friend, to the awareness that spiritual maturity has not been left up to you to figure out or to achieve, but that the third member of the Trinity himself, the Holy Spirit, is tenaciously at work in you. What He has begun, He is faithful to bring to pass.

In this final chapter, I want to challenge you to receive the call to a revolution. It's the revolution to redeem and restore the orphan planet back to the Father. It's the revolution Jesus was sent to inaugurate and the Holy Spirit was sent to facilitate. It's the mission of the Father, Son, and Spirit to bring many sons to glory. You and I have been fully deputized to join in the campaign. To have a revolution that turns men's hearts to love we will need what every revolution needs: willing warriors (in this case, fathers), a redefining of the terms, and supernatural resources that negate the opposition's strength. Let's explore these.

Willing Warriors: Sonship Requires Fathers

The rash of school shootings and ongoing murder in the inner cities has raised the social awareness of a deteriorating condition and the all-too-shallow efforts to find the quick solution. Is it guns? Is it a lack of gun laws? Is it lack of control in the schools? Is it the broken family system? Is it God's judgment on America? Or is it a father problem? Warren Farrell says:

> Every one of the school shootings have one thing in common; sons growing up in fatherless homes. Either minimal involvement with dads or no involvement with dads. No involvement usually comes after divorce, and the 51 percent of women under thirty who are raising children without father-involvement. Sometimes that father-involvement exists in the beginning, but after two years the father drops out completely. That combination accounts for all school shooters; Adam Lamsa, Steven Paddock, Nicolas Cruz … they are all Dad-deprived boys. The solution is father-involvement.[66]

The connection between troubled sons and the lack of fathers has been well documented. However, the lack of father involvement begs the question, Why are men afraid to father? What is going on with men in our culture? Sociologists, educators, and politicians will suggest camping, sports leagues, and quality time as a solution. No doubt healthy personal relationships are at the core of how mankind is made in God's image and the foundation of emotional health. But the crux of the *Abba* series is to speak to the foundation of emotional health, which is spiritual health. The transformational work of the Spirit within us does not begin at the emotional level, but in the spirit of the person.

Guard your heart with all diligence, for out of it flows the forces of life.
Proverbs 4:23

Fathers don't produce whole and healthy sons. *Whole and healthy fathers* (and let's not forget mothers) produce whole and healthy sons and daughters. Spiritual health produces emotional and relational health, not the other way around. The purpose of our study has been to get to the very root of all human brokenness and the many issues that arise from it. The root is the orphan spirit and its alienation from God and from one another. Spiritual transformation by the Holy Spirit—the inside job of transformation from orphans to heirs—is the only lasting solution to the human dilemma.

We are using natural situations and problems to describe the more real spiritual ones. Spiritual fathers are needed to raise up spiritual sons and daughters. I am convinced that most of our current church programs have proven ineffective to produce much more than church attenders. This is not meant as a criticism, but to highlight that fathering requires someone willing to discipline sons, and reciprocally, sons who will submit to spiritual fathers and live. The current competitive environment for church attendance practically paralyzes church leadership from administering the kind of disciplines required to produce sons, but the Holy Spirit knows how to enlist willing warriors. The second task is to help those willing warriors embrace revolutionary thinking that counters the way of the world, which requires redefining the terms.

Sonship Redefines the Terms

If anyone knows about revolution, it's Karl Marx. Perhaps his brand could only be called "failed revolution" because he had to slaughter as many as 100 million people to implement his campaign. One who studied Marx well and has had massive impact upon the American scene is Saul Alinsky. His book, *Rules For Radicals*, has been the playbook for subversives for the past fifty-plus years. He says, "Remember, there are no such things as rules for revolution, any more than there are rules for love or peace; but there are rules for radicals that want to change the world."[67] One of

Spiritual fathers are needed to raise up spiritual sons and daughters.

these rules that radicals have used for millennia is that the first order of business is to redefine terms, to hijack the language to mean something other than what it traditionally meant, to make what was formerly unthinkable acceptable. Think of how the words "gay," "viable," "hot," "porn," "Christian," or "socialist" have all come to mean something far different from their original usage. Things that were taboo or shameful to culture are eventually made acceptable and normalized by humanizing the behavior and redefining the terms.

This tactic goes back to the Garden where Satan attempts to redefine God's term "to die." He supplants the truth with a lie—a slightly modified but distorted version of the real.

> *And he* [the serpent] *said to the woman, "Has God indeed said, 'You shall not eat of every tree of the garden'?" … Then the serpent said to the woman, "You will not surely die."*
> Genesis 3:1, 4

Because Adam and Eve did not die physically on the day of their disobedience, the lie seemed to be validated; but they did die.

We see the same tactic used in the Babylonian captivity of Israel. The first thing the Babylonians did to the Jewish subjects was give them Babylonian names, and with the new names, altered identities. Hananiah, Azariah, and Mishael, the finest of the finest of Israel were renamed Shadrach, Meshach, and Abed-Nego (all three names mean "slave of" or "servant of" someone else). Daniel's name was changed to Belteshazzar. His Hebrew name means "God is judge, or judge of God." His new Babylonian name means "protector of the King." How subtle! Whereas Daniel was one who would interpret dreams, shun evil, and faithfully worship God by the Spirit of God, the task of protecting Nebuchadnezzar would have been an elite position. Considering the wealth, pomp, and prestige of that kingdom, it surely must have been a tempting trade-off.

> *But Daniel purposed in his heart that he would not defile himself.*
> Daniel 1:8

The tactics of radicals have historically been used in opposition to the Father's mission, but it doesn't have to be that way. We are called to a radical mission of restoration, a radical mission of love. Ours is a radical mission to destroy the works of the enemy. We are in a spiritual battle and must learn to engage it as sons, not as orphans.

> *For the weapons of our warfare are not carnal but mighty in God for*
> *pulling down strongholds, casting down arguments and every high*
> *thing that exalts itself against the knowledge of God, bringing every*
> *thought into captivity to the obedience of Christ, and being ready to*
> *punish all disobedience when your obedience is fulfilled.*
> 2 Corinthians 10:4-6

Jesus as a Radical

Jesus was a radical in the sense that He exposed deception by speaking truth. He was such a threat to the existing religious establishment that they sought to kill Him. It's difficult for most Christians to see Jesus as a true radical in His religious culture, but that is exactly what He represented to the religious ruling class—the Pharisees. They represented a form of Judaism that had added four-hundred new laws since Malachi (which Jesus called "the traditions of the elders"). This Judaism was centered in power and partnership with the Roman State, and was choking out the life of the true worship of God (Mark 7:3-13).

The rise of Pharisaical Judaism during the Intertestamental Period (350 BC to Jesus' day) became consumed with more and more laws. As a side note, when there's an absence of the Spirit, humanity will grasp for behaviors, rules, and law to fill the void. The Pharisees had convinced all Jews to submit to "the traditions of the elders," so when Jesus came on the scene they were measuring Him, not by the revelation of God but by the religious traditions of men. They questioned Him over details such as, "Why don't your disciples wash their hands?" (Mark 7:5).

There are those who say that Jesus must be understood through the lens of Moses, but Jesus actually came to reinterpret Moses for those who had a wrong view of God. There are those who say Jesus can only be understood through the lens of rabbinical Judaism, but Jesus actually reinterpreted rabbinical Judaism, teaching and speaking, not as the rabbis of His day but as one having authority. Rabbinical Judaism had become grossly distorted and political. There are those who say Jesus actually raised the bar and made the law more difficult to adhere to, but Jesus actually reinterpreted the very meaning for which the Law was given. In other words, He redefined the terms for being reconciled to God. He was doing what revolutionaries do.

Jesus Redefines Common Understanding

Listen to how Jesus redefines the religious terms of His day: "You have heard it said … but I say to you …"

> *You have heard that it was said to those of old, "You shall not murder,*
> *and whoever murders will be in danger of the judgment."'*
> ***But I say** to you that whoever is angry with his brother without*
> *a cause shall be in danger of the judgment.*
> Matthew 5:21-22

He redefines murder as more than a physical act of violence, but a hatred of spirit that does violence to God's relational nature of wholeness-in-love.

> *You have heard that it was said to those of old, "You shall not commit*
> *adultery." **But I say** to you that whoever looks at a woman to lust for her*
> *has already committed adultery with her in his heart.*
> Matthew 5:27-28

Again, Jesus is not just "raising the bar" of holiness, He is revealing that holiness is about wholeness. It's an internal reality with an outward expression. Holiness is relational wholeness. As such, adultery is not just about the act of sex outside of marriage, but about breaking covenant with one's spouse. That spiritual separation can happen long before an extra-marital affair does. Jesus is pointing to God's wiring for human wholeness in relationship, not just a sin-management system that keeps one from acting out. See if you can grasp the real issue of relational wholeness that this radical Jesus is calling for in the following references:

> *Again you have heard that it was said to those of old, "You shall not swear*
> *falsely, but shall perform your oaths to the Lord." **But I say to you,***
> *do not swear at all: neither by heaven, for it is God's throne;*
> *nor by the earth, for it is His footstool.*
> Matthew 5:33-35

*You have heard that it was said, "An eye for an eye and a tooth for a tooth." **But I tell you** not to resist an evil person. But whoever slaps you on your right cheek, turn the other to him also.*
Matthew 5:38-39

The Holy Spirit has come to redefine the terms that you have used to measure yourself.

*You have heard that it was said, "You shall love your neighbor and hate your enemy." **But I say** to you, love your enemies, bless those who curse you, do good to those who hate you, and pray for those who spitefully use you and persecute you.*
Matthew 5:43-44

You might be asking, "How does this pertain to the *Abba Formation*—the work of Spirit in my spiritual transformation?" In every way. The Holy Spirit has come to redefine the terms that you have used to measure yourself. The Holy Spirit is showing you how the Father sees you and revealing your real name instead of the many labels that the world has given you. You are not Belteshazzar, but Daniel—one who can see and judge by the Spirit. You are not Cephas, but Peter—a rock of stability. You are not an orphan, but a son.

Transformation: Seeing Old Things in a New Way

One of the keys to your own spiritual transformation is your willingness to have truth and reality redefined. The greatest challenges to our transformation can be those traditions we learn in church that have the stamp of spiritual authority on them. For example, Jesus tells His disciples:

There is nothing outside a person that by going into him can defile him, but the things that come out of a person are what defile him.
Mark 7:15 (ESV)

The "tradition of the elders" had redefined the food laws (hygiene laws) of the Old Testament into measurements of holiness (spiritual righteousness). The term "unclean" was never meant to be a spiritual

One of the keys to your own spiritual transformation is your willingness to have truth and reality redefined.

label that ostracized and isolated people from God or each other. On the contrary, it was meant to protect God's people from diseases and contagions transferred by germs. Jesus reinterpreted the way God's instructions had been understood. Jesus redefines their terms and declares all foods clean. This is radical!

> *His disciples asked him about the parable. And he said to them, "Then are you also without understanding? Do you not see that whatever goes into a person from outside cannot defile him, since it enters not his heart but his stomach, and is expelled?" (Thus he declared all foods clean.)*
> Mark 7:17-19 (ESV)

Almost ten years later, Peter was still holding on to the traditions of his Jewish upbringing. He could not understand God's heart for all people. To make this connection clear I need to give you some background. Stay with me.

Mark's Gospel is known as "the memoirs of Peter." What we read in Mark are Peter's recollection of the works and sayings of Jesus as Peter told them to Mark. Peter was present when Jesus said, "All foods are clean."[68] He heard Jesus say it, but almost ten years later he still didn't understand the application. In Acts 10, we read that Peter was on a rooftop praying (think of a second-floor porch or patio), and the Lord gave him a vision of a sheet being let down with "unclean animals" (Acts 10:9-16). Peter responds to the Lord by saying, "Lord, You know I have never eaten unclean foods." He was still obeying the food laws of the Jews.

Did you know you can be so committed to fighting for right doctrine that you miss the wind of the Spirit and your own transformation? Peter was so stuck in the Mosaic Law (and the legalistic pressures of Jerusalem) that the Lord had to show him the vision three times before he could "get it." The vision wasn't even about food laws. That was not the issue. The "unclean foods" represented all nations. Jesus was telling Peter, by the Holy Spirit, that Jesus shed His blood for all nations, tribes and tongues, so they can all be reconciled to the Father. Jesus was calling Peter to proclaim the Gospel to the Gentiles.

Peter went with the Gentile men who had come looking for him. In opposition to the "traditions of the elders," he preached to the Gentiles in Cornelius' house. The Holy Spirit was poured out for the first time upon non-Jews. Notice that when Peter is preaching to them he declares:

> *You yourselves know how unlawful it is for a Jew to associate with or to*
> *visit anyone of another nation, but God has shown me that I should not*
> *call any person common or unclean.*
>
> Acts 10:28[69]

Peter finally understood that it was not ultimately about what kind of foods we eat, but whether or not we think about people the same way God does.

Jesus had to redefine the terms "holy," "clean," "unclean" and "common" for Peter. The reality is, Peter had lived in Jerusalem since Jesus' resurrection, and the religious pressures prevalent in that city had an ongoing impact on Peter's ability to live in the transformation that Jesus had already declared. Satan can use our surroundings and the prevailing view (whether it's a worldly view or a religious view) to thwart our freedom in sonship.[70] One specific way our religious thinking blinds us to Jesus' revolutionary transformation is the idea of keeping the commandments.

What Does It Mean to Keep the Commandments?

We should grasp, by virtue of the rest of the New Testament, that pleasing God is no longer about conforming our behavior to a certain set of laws or commands. Paul plainly says:

> *So let no one judge you in food or in drink, or regarding a festival*
> *or a new moon or Sabbaths, which are a shadow of things to come, but the*
> *substance is of Christ. … Therefore, if you died with Christ from the basic*
> *principles of the world, why, as though living in the world, do you subject*
> *yourselves to regulations—"Do not touch, do not taste, do not handle," …*
> *according to the commandments and doctrines of men?*
>
> Colossians 2:16-17, 20-22

Also consider Paul's contrast to keeping the commandments of the Law and living the life of the Spirit.

> *But now we have been delivered from the*
> *law, having died to what we were held by,*
> *so that we should serve in the newness of the*
> *Spirit and not in the oldness of the letter.*
>
> Romans 7:6

Jesus had to redefine the terms "holy," "clean," "unclean" and "common" for Peter.

When we read where Jesus says, "keep My commandments" (John 14:15, 21; 15:10) it sounds like the Old Testament command to obey the letter of the Law. Our minds suddenly revert to an Old Testament system of behavior management, but Jesus is redefining the terms. The word "keep" here is very interesting. In the original language, it's the word *tereō*, which refers to something different from mere obedience or compliant behavior. The word *tereō* has a sense of a careful, watchful protection with the idea of cherishing or valuing; to cherish, watch over, or value. The best way I know to express this idea is how I feel when I have any sense that one of my daughters might be in danger. It is a watchful, careful, almost jealous, protection of a thing. Let me illustrate this important New Testament redefinition of an important Old Testament term.

My young family and I were in New York City several years ago on vacation, walking down one of the busy streets of Manhattan. We stopped to look at a menu outside a restaurant to decide whether to eat there. The consensus was to move on. As we started walking again, I quickly counted heads and found that my youngest, Lauren, who was eight at the time, was missing. We were in Manhattan and I couldn't see my little girl. My heart went through my throat. In a split second my thoughts were racing, my heart palpitating. I thought to myself, "She probably didn't know that we stopped to look at the window, and she's probably still walking. She must be caught up in a crowd, so I bet she's just a bit farther this way." Thoughts of impending danger flashed. I've never felt so much fear! "My little girl is gone." I took off running, full of adrenalin. I looked across the next intersection and I saw her in the middle of a crowd, being moved along in a mob of pedestrians boarding a city bus!

The panic increased. I thought, "If she gets on that bus and the doors close, I may never see her again." With everything I had I yelled, "Lauren!!!!!" I ran unaware and unafraid of the traffic. Suddenly she turned around, and then realized that she was not with her family. Fear came over her face, and then, just as fast as it came, it was gone. She brightened up, grabbed my hand, and I brought her back to the family. For the next week and a half, I don't think we ever let go of each other's hand. Seriously, for that whole vacation I had little fingerprints deeply embedded in my palm. Do you think I know what it means to watch carefully, jealously, protectively?

The word *tereō* conveys this covetous, jealous, protective care. When Jesus says, "keep My commandments," He is not asking us to routinely obey a rule. He is saying, "Cherish every word I speak, because in My words are spirit and life" (John 6:63).[71] The key to living as a son is not some stressed, religious obedience, but being close enough in proximity to the Father that you hear every whisper He speaks to you and you keep it like it's the last words you'll ever hear from Him. Is it a fearful thing? Yes, in a good sense it is a fearful thing: you don't ever want to be away from Father's presence. You keep it. You cherish it. Maybe it's cherishing-on-steroids.

If you keep My commandments, you will abide in My love, just as I have kept My Father's commandments and abide in His love.

John 15:10

Jesus and Paul redefine what it means to "keep the commandments." It's not a rule-keeping, behavioral straight-jacket, but a heart that passionately protects and cherishes relationship. I love the way The Message paraphrases Paul's words:

The person who believes God, is set right by God—and that's the real life. Rule-keeping does not naturally evolve into living by faith, but only perpetuates itself in more and more rule-keeping, a fact observed in Scripture: "The one who does these things [rule-keeping] continues to live by them." ... For if any kind of rule-keeping had power to create life in us, we would certainly have gotten it by this time ... I am emphatic about this. The moment any one of you submits to circumcision or any other rule-keeping system, at that same moment Christ's hard-won gift of freedom is squandered.

Galatians 3:12, 22; 5:2 (MSG)

Keeping His commandments is no longer mere obedience to a code of ethics of behavioral standards. It is cherishing the words of Jesus in a relational way by the indwelling Holy Spirit. This is the byproduct of the *Abba Formation*. As a radical revolutionary, Jesus reinterpreted the Law, reinterpreted Rabbinic Judaism, and redefined what it means to keep the commandments ... why would we go back to a former interpretation?

Are you living in this reality? I am experiencing a stirring, a hunger; something like a home-sickness that says, "God, I want all of You that I can get here and now. I don't want to just wait until I get to heaven. Jesus, You said that You would come and manifest Yourself to me. I want whatever that is, and as much of it as I can get right now." My sense is that this manifesting Himself by the indwelling Spirit is this synchronizing kind of a life that Jesus modeled for us. What if God's intent is to calibrate our lives to the life of Jesus so much that people can look into our lives and see the Father, the same way Jesus showed us the Father?

> *But the Helper, the Holy Spirit, whom the Father will send in*
> *My name, He will teach you all things, and bring to*
> *your remembrance all things that I said to you.*
>
> John 14:26

Do you want to have a revolution? Jesus' intention was nothing less than a total takeover of the world, to fill this orphan planet with the Father's love. The Father sent His Son to bring many sons to glory. This is truly revolutionary. As we said at the onset, this revolution requires willing warriors, a redefinition of terms, and supernatural resources.

Before we leave the Revolutionary's idea of redefining terms, let's underscore what has been said. Over time Christianity, especially in the West, has lost the original intent of Jesus' radical transformation of the old to the new. Jesus redefined the Old Testament notions about rule-keeping righteousness, the primacy of doing before being, "unclean" as a spiritual label, holiness as behavior, discipleship as practices, and so on. If the goal was just to get folks to Heaven, there would have been no reason for Jesus to send the Holy Spirit to live within the believer. Jesus didn't pour out His Spirit upon the Church so we could "do" witnessing, but rather that we would "be witnesses" by our passionate spirituality, showing the world a living definition of love, discipleship, church, abiding, fullness, worship, and community. The goal of the *Abba Formation* is to produce nothing less than multitudes that live, love, think, talk, and walk like Jesus because they are, in fact, filled with the very Spirit with which Jesus was and is filled.

Every revolution needs these three components: willing warriors, a redefining of the terms, and resources that negate the opposition's strength. To wrap up the essential strategy of Jesus' revolutionary movement we will look at supernatural resources that negate the opposition's strength.

Supernatural Resources: Sonship Contends for the Spirit

Less than a week ago, I was awakened early with these words coming up from my spirit, "You must contend for the things of the Spirit. The ways of the Spirit are free, but not automatically passed down from generation to generation. You must apprehend it for yourself and keep fanning the flame." I have heard these words about contending for the Spirit many times before—and each time there is a sense of urgency. After praying for a while I opened my Bible to Leviticus 24 (the daily assigned reading in my Bible reading plan). Here is what I read:

> *The Lord spoke to Moses, saying, "Command the people of Israel*
> *to bring you pure oil from beaten olives for the lamp, that a light may*
> *be kept burning regularly. Outside the veil of the testimony,*
> *in the tent of meeting, Aaron shall arrange it from evening to*
> *morning before the Lord regularly. It shall be a statute forever*
> *throughout your generations. He shall arrange the lamps*
> *on the lampstand of pure gold before the Lord regularly.*
> Leviticus 24:1-4 (ESV)

These verses underscored the word that had awakened me. The oil from the olives represents the Holy Spirit and the anointing/unction that He ministers to and through the believer. The fact that these olives are "beaten" (other translations use crushed or pressed), speaks of an aggressive, percussive process required to extract the oil. What is the oil used for? Nothing less than providing fuel for the light of the Holy Place. Since there were no windows through which natural light could enter the room, the candlestick provided the only light in the Holy Place. That is to say, the flames from that candlestick represented the supernatural illumination or revelation of the Holy Spirit.

In this passage the Lord is charging Aaron (and the priests to follow) with the responsibility to keep the wicks trimmed, the lamps fueled with oil, and the candles burning so the light would never go out in the Holy Place. This is not a passive ministry. The candle doesn't keep burning indefinitely simply because it had been lit once before. These verses prompted me to ask, "Is there any occurrence in Scripture where we see the flame going out or the candlestick not properly maintained?" Yes. In fact, Jesus warned the seven New Testament churches of Asia Minor that there were certain things that had been left undone, and if these issues were not tended to—if they didn't repent and return to their first love—He would "remove the lampstand from its place" (Rev. 2:5). Unfortunately, none of those seven churches exist today. We don't know the exact reasons, but it's evident that the light went out.

I believe the Lord is saying that the work of the Spirit in us, the *Abba Formation*, is more than an optional extra for the Church and more than just necessary spiritual growth. There is a daily contending for life in the Spirit. The olives must be crushed and the oil extracted. A pressing is also required. Yes, God's love is unconditional. This is not about whether we are loved or not, but about millions of orphans who don't know the way back to Father's house.

The Holy Spirit is the oil, the flame, the candle disbursing the revelation of the Lord (His mind, will, and purpose) in our spirits.

> *The spirit of man is the candle of the Lord.*
>   Proverbs 20:27

We must contend for the candle to stay lit. As mentioned in the previous chapter, every day we must poke a hole in the membrane that seemingly separates the physical world and the spiritual world.

Poking a Hole in the Spiritual-Physical Divide

The fact that the Bible uses so many physical metaphors like candles, flames, and light to speak of spiritual reality means that the two worlds are not as far apart as we might think. Imagine that there is a large elastic membrane, like a very thin wall, separating the physical world from the spiritual world. Earth's reality is on this side of the membrane, and Heaven's reality is just inches away, but on the other side. Now imagine that you can, with some effort, push your hand through the elastic membrane and grab something of Heaven and bring it back to this physical realm. In a sense, you poke a hole in the membrane—you press through the veil—to get something that is otherwise reserved for another time.

In a very real sense, this is how we contend for the things of the Spirit. We know that we are citizens of two kingdoms and live simultaneously in two dimensions. We live a natural human life, and at the same time are seated with Him in heavenly places in Christ Jesus (Eph. 1:20). Our life is hid with Christ in God (Col. 3:3), and at the same time "living epistles known and read of all men" (2 Cor. 3:1-3). Paul describes the two worlds this way:

Any way that you bring the reality of the Spirit dimension into this physical realm, you have brought the eternal to bear down on the temporal.

We do not look at the things which are seen, but at the things which are not seen. For the things which are seen are temporary [natural, physical]*, but the things which are not seen are eternal* [spiritual].

2 Corinthians 4:18

Jesus demonstrated what it means to bring the spiritual reality into the physical world. He would heal the sick, cast out devils, even raise the dead, and say, "The Kingdom of God is at hand (within reach and available)." He modeled a spiritual revolution with spiritual weapons, not natural ones. Therefore, the way we fight begins by poking a hole in the membrane that separates the physical and the spiritual. How do we do that? In short, any way that you bring the reality of the Spirit dimension into this physical realm, you have brought the eternal to bear down on the temporal. You can do this with your words, with your actions, and with your interactions with others. Let's explore a few examples.

Lifting Your Hands

David understood the power of bringing the supernatural into the natural. He said:

Let my prayer be set before You as incense,
The lifting up of my hands [natural, physical]
as the evening sacrifice be [supernatural, spiritual]

Psalm 141:2

David understood a spiritual principle that would be disclosed several hundred years later by Paul,

Do not present your members [physical body] *as instruments of unrighteousness to sin, but present ... your members as instruments* [hoplon: weapons] *of righteousness to God.*

Romans 6:13

Aaron and Hur held up Moses' hands and poked a hole in the spiritual-physical divide until the enemies were routed. Moses raised a rod over the Red Sea, the priests waved the early harvest sheaves, Jesus raised five loaves and two fish, and God raised His only Son on a cross and poked a hole in the veil by His flesh. God will use the lifting of your hands as spiritual weapons against the enemy. That's how you poke a hole in it. And you can do that every day.

Lifting our hands in worship is much more than a style of worship or even a show of spirituality. Paul exhorted Timothy as a young pastor to have the men, wherever they gather to lift their hands:

What I want mostly is for men to pray—not shaking angry fists at enemies but raising holy hands to God.

1 Timothy 2:8 (MSG)

Why would Paul, using a gender-specific term in the original language, encourage Timothy to have the men in the assembly raise their hands when they pray? Because he understands something about poking a hole in the membrane that seems to separate the physical and the spiritual. God takes the weak things of this world to confound the mighty. He has ordained praise—the many expressions of it—to stop the enemy. When men learn to use spiritual weapons instead of physical force, they gain the advantage in the spiritual battle. Also, if the males set the tone, the rest of the family will do the same. Let's look at another way that we can bring the reality of Heaven to bear upon the earth.

Lifting Your Voice

Do you realize that it has been ordained (set in order in the spiritual realm) that the praises of God, coming from the mouths of spiritual infants, stop the enemy in his tracks and silence his accusations?

Out of the mouth of babes and nursing infants
You have ordained strength, Because of Your enemies,
That You may silence the enemy and the avenger.

Psalm 8:2

Interestingly, when Jesus quotes this verse in the New Testament, He replaces the word "strength" with the word "praise." What does this mean? Praise lifted up on the earth-side (the physical dimension) taps into strength coming from the spiritual dimension. Heaven's power is available to those who simply praise Him. Heaven is ready to releases warriors against the enemy when we praise. David also said:

Let the saints be joyful in glory;
Let them sing aloud on their beds.
Let the high praises of God be in their mouth,
And a two-edged sword in their hand,
To execute vengeance on the nations,
And punishments on the peoples;
To bind their kings with chains,
And their nobles with fetters of iron;
To execute on them the written judgment—
This honor have all His saints.
Praise the Lord!

Psalm 149:5-9

David knew something in the Old Testament that a lot of saints still don't understand in the New Testament. You can sit on your couch or lie in your bed and sing, and God will use your voice to fight your battles and defeat the enemy! His praise in your mouth becomes a two-edged sword in God's hands. That is something physical [a song] becoming spiritual [a sword]. That's how you poke a hole in it.

Jehoshaphat put the singers out front, Joshua marched around Jericho, then shouted on command, and poked a hole in the veil between the physical and spiritual. Elijah prayed earnestly that it would rain, and poked a hole in the heavens. Jesus spoke to a barren fig tree and it withered from the roots. Paul and Silas sang praises to God at midnight, and poked a hole in it, and the earth shook and the prison bars opened. Your voice is your address in the spirit dimension, and it is also the spear that can

Your words and conversation about God open people to the spiritual dimension. poke a hole in the veil between heaven and earth. I have to say that again—your voice is the spear that can poke a hole in the membrane between heaven and earth. Here is yet another way for your spiritual transformation to have an impact beyond yourself.

Having God-Conversations with Others

Moses told Pharaoh, "Let my people go." He had to declare it several times, but Israel plundered Egypt and there is no natural way to explain it. Nathan spoke convicting words to David, "Thou art the man," and a spirit of repentance came upon David. Jesus spoke to demon possessed people, the evil spirits came out, and they were delivered. He poked a hole in their torment! Paul spoke words to the Philippian jailer and there was an entrance created for him and his entire household into the kingdom of God.

Have you ever had an experience where you were talking with someone else about the things of the Lord, and suddenly God used their words to speak to you? Do you know that God has used your words to speak to others as well? Your words and conversation about God opens people to the spiritual dimension. Did you know that you have the power to poke a hole in that invisible membrane that keeps people blind to the spiritual reality of God's love? What if you actually took to heart that the only thing separating them from God was for someone to come along and poke a hole in that veil? This is why Chiqui and I make a habit of asking our waiter or waitress if we can pray for them when we pray for our food. It opens their heart to the reality of God's love. Many powerful conversations and prayers have come through that little "poke," which involves having God conversations and partnering with the Holy Spirit in His gifts. This is yet another way in which you can have spiritual impact. Here is another outward expression of the internal working of your transformation.

The Gifts of the Spirit

The gifts of the Spirit are readily available to the believer who will simply open the conversation, looking for a bridge into people's hearts. Words of knowledge, words of wisdom, prophecy, healings, and the other manifestations of the Spirit are just on the other side of that veil and ready to be used. Reach through the veil, receive from the Holy Spirit, and bring the love of God from the spiritual into the natural. Let them "taste and see that the Lord is good" (Ps. 34:8).

You have to learn to poke a hole into the heavenlies every day.

A couple of weeks ago Chiqui and I were eating in a Thai restaurant and, as usual, the waitress brought us our menus and introduced herself. After she left our table I said to Chiqui, "She has an interesting accent. I wonder where she is from." Chiqui said, "It sounds Eastern European." I didn't give it any more thought, but when she came back to the table with our waters I abruptly said, "Are you from Moldova?" Chiqui looked at me like I had just come from the moon. I don't think either of us had ever talked about Moldova, and I couldn't have pointed it on a map. The waitress was shocked. She said, "How did you know? No one has ever guessed that I am from Moldova—Russia maybe, but never Moldova."

I didn't know where she was from, but when I opened my mouth, the Holy Spirit gave me those words and made a divine connection. All night, Marinella kept stopping by our table and talking to us. The manifestation of a word of knowledge—supernaturally imparted—opened the door for a divine opportunity. Through that simple act she knew she was on God's radar and felt His love.

If you are interested in partnering with God in a supernaturally-natural way, read my book, *The Gifts of the Spirit For a New Generation*. The Holy Spirit is much more interested in the Marinellas of the world than you and me. He just needs some willing partners to "poke a hole in it." You might say, "I would be too afraid to do anything like that." I understand that, without learning to live in the Spirit ourselves, it seems spooky to think about doing the works of Jesus that we read about in Scripture, or even praying for a server at a restaurant, but here is the key: You have to learn to poke a hole into the heavenlies every day. Why? Because there is no such thing as internal spiritual transformation that is not eventually demonstrated in outward expression.

A Global Revolution

The challenge we face in this so-called "Post-Christian" West is that we have normalized Christianity. We lost the sense of revolution that Jesus came to ignite. Listen to His words:

The Holy Spirit is tenaciously downloading the Father's purpose, the Son's pleasure, and His power into you so that even creation sees the rising of the sons of God.

I came to send fire on the earth,
and how I wish it were already kindled!

Luke 12:49

We have given in to the notions of success on the world's terms, so we are content with "doing church" instead of making disciples—but Jesus has fire in His hand.

We must reclaim Jesus' own sense of filling the whole world with the good news that orphans can be sons again. Let's not forget that He has always intended "the whole world" to mean everyone. Though Jesus never ministered more than thirty miles from His birthplace, He was always aware that the Father's business is a global mission. Every step Jesus took and every word He spoke was intended to prepare His disciples to launch a global revolution. Listen to Jesus as He prays for us:

I do not pray for these [disciples] *alone,*
but also for those who will believe in Me through their word.

John 17:20

After His resurrection He commissions us ...

All authority has been given to Me in heaven and on earth.
*Go therefore and make disciples of **all the nations**, baptizing them*
in the name [realm and operation] of the Father and of the Son
and of the Holy Spirit, teaching them to observe all things that I have
commanded you; and lo, I am with you always,
even to the end of the age.

Matthew 28:18-20

His intention was and is for His disciples to be revolutionaries, pioneers, risk-takers, and trail-blazers, and the Holy Spirit is tenaciously downloading the Father's purpose, the Son's pleasure, and His power into you so that even creation sees the rising of the sons of God.

Taking the Call Seriously

How did Jesus' vision for the world burn so intensely in the hearts of His original team? Why were they so willing to be dispersed to Africa, India, Asia and Europe to take this good news revolution to prodigal sons and daughters? I don't believe it had anything to do with His curriculum, His teaching style, or His personality. The Holy Spirit that filled Him, moved Him with compassion, and anointed Him to heal, bind up, and set free, is the same Holy Spirit that transforms you and me into loving revolutionaries that live to set the captives free.

Where is the passion to go to the nations to tell orphans that they can return to Father's house? The Holy Spirit is looking for sons and daughters who have learned how to make the connection between the natural and spiritual dimension—to bring a bit of Heaven to earth. May many hear the call of God to personal transformation. Moreover, may many heed the call to transformation so they can join in the Father's mission and bring home those who are living as orphans. When we go, whether across the street or around the world, let's declare the good news that our Father is other-centered, infinite love, and His arms are open wide. May we press in continually for our own transformation, and then bring many others into the same experience by the Holy Spirit.

What Have We Said?

Jesus came to the earth and was clothed in humanity to start, not a new religion, but a revolution of sonship. He came to effect a radical restoration of sons to the Father. He came to turn the hearts of fathers to the children and children to fathers—more specifically, to turn the hearts of orphans to the Father.

One of the primary rules of revolutionaries is to redefine existing terms. Jesus reinterpreted Moses, the Law, the commandments, rabbinical ministry, and the understanding of the terms "holy," "clean," "unclean" and "common."

One of the keys to our own spiritual transformation is our willingness to have truth and reality redefined. The work of the Spirit is to redefine our view of God and ourselves as Father and sons. This is the *Abba Formation*.

Personal transformation is not just for personal comfort, but to be free to be other-centered. Any way that we bring the reality of the Spirit dimension into this physical realm, we have brought the eternal into the temporal, and made the Father's love available to others. We can do this with our words, with our actions, and with our interactions with others.

For Jesus, this has always been a global mission. His desire has always been to fill the whole earth with the knowledge of the glory of the Lord, and He is doing this by giving His Spirit to sons and daughters.

PRAYER

Father, I pray that You would teach me to contend for the Spirit in my life. Teach me, Holy Spirit, how to "poke a hole" in the membrane that seems to separate the physical and spiritual world so the Kingdom of God can come. Teach me how to stay connected to You, and how to stay sensitive and aware of Your presence. Teach me how to lean into to people rather than look past them. Teach me to see them the way You do. I ask You to continue to kindle a fire in my own heart and give me boldness to give away what You pour into me. Make me a revolutionary in a religious world that clamors for the status quo. Holy Spirit, I welcome You to redefine the terms of my life. I welcome You to redefine what being a disciple looks like, what being son looks like, and what keeping Your commandments, cherishing Your words is all about. I invite You to continue redefining how I see myself by how the Father sees me. As You are forming the life and nature of Abba in me, make me an instrument in the lives of others. Make me useful in Your revolution to bring many sons to glory. I trust You. I love You. I belong to You. Amen.

GROUP DISCUSSION

1. In what ways could we say Jesus was a revolutionary toward the religious establishment of His day? Why did the Pharisees hate Him as they did?

2. In what ways did Jesus redefine the terms of relationship with God, as the Jewish people in that day had come to know Him?

3. How is "keeping (*tereō*: cherishing, watching over, guarding) the commandments" different in the New Covenant than under the Older Covenant?

4. Why is the penetration of the spiritual realm into the natural realm so important for bringing orphans back to the Father?

5. What are some of the ways we can "poke a hole" in the seeming separation, to make the Kingdom of Heaven available now?

End Notes

[1] Francis Chan, *Forgotten God: Reversing Our Tragic Neglect of the Holy Spirit* (Colorado Springs, David C. Cook, 2009), and *Remembering the Forgotten God* (Colorado Springs: David C. Cook Publishing, 2010).

[2] Gordon Fee, *Paul, The Spirit and the People of God* (Grand Rapids: Baker Academic, 1996), 90.

[3] Ibid.

[4] See Mephibosheth's story in 2 Samuel 4 and 2 Samuel 9.

[5] There are some in the Arab world today that might consider the U.S. as "the devil." They assume (because of the lies they have believed) that Americans would kill every Arab if we found them. The Jews have believed (in the more orthodox circles) that Americans and Christians hate Jews and that if Americans ever have a chance they will slaughter Jews. That sounds so preposterous to my ears, but there are people who deeply believe it.

[6] City of refuge: Under the old covenant law, if you had killed or maimed someone, their immediate relatives could exact revenge if they find you. So, in God's mercy, He set up cities of refuge where a perpetrator could go hide in that city. If you had wounded somebody, they or their family could come get you, but they would have to come into a city full of thieves; a city full of robbers and murderers. And if you dared go in there, you'd be on your own.

[7] Merrill F. Unger, *Unger's Bible Dictionary* (Chicago: Moody Press, 1979).

[8] It should be noted that Paul never calls the Church the "People of the Book" (*graphetikoi*), or even "People of the Word" (*logostikoi* or *rhematikoi*), but he calls the Church a *pneumatikoi*, the People of the Spirit.

[9] Gerhard Kittel and Gerhard Friedrich, eds., *Theological Dictionary of the New Testament*, (Grand Rapids: Eerdmans, 1985), 467. There are difficulties knowing whether Paul is asserting that spiritual truths are being compared/explained to spiritual people, spiritual realities combined with spiritual words, or spiritual things with other spiritual things. What we do know from the context is that people that don't have the Spirit do not have access to the thoughts of the Spirit, and that words in the Spirit are the process used to compare and convey. See also Gordon Fee, *GOD's Empowering Presence: The Holy Spirit in the Letters of Paul* (Peabody, MA: Hendrickson, 1994), 104-105.

[10] The mechanically-minded person would also want to think about the fact that when a vehicle has to turn left or right, the wheels on one side of

the car are turning at a different speed than the others, thus the "gear differential" allows nimble movement in the turns. The Holy Spirit, synchronizing God's plans, thoughts and purposes in our spirits also makes us nimble to makes course adjustment with God's plans. We don't have to be paralyzed with constant fear that we may or may not be in the "perfect" will of God. His Spirit knows how to help us make minor and subtle adjustments.

[11]Gordon Fee, a leading Pentecostal theologian and scholar uses a capital "S" followed by a forward slash and a small "s" when referring to the Holy Spirit at work in the human spirit, since in the Greek language Paul refers to them working in union with one another. Thus S/spirit seems an effective way to communicate this idea in English.

[12]It is significant to note that Paul's letter to the Romans is, in essence, the complete treatise of His theology since he had never been with the Rome believers before and was seeking an entrance and support by them. When Paul summarizes the issue of how both Jew and Greek are not only redeemed, but fulfill the Law in righteousness, and are made one, the "*Abba Cry*" is the process he refers to that makes that personal transformation a reality (Rom. 8), whereby they are free from the mastery of sin. When writing to the Galatians, he is dealing with the issue of Judaizers tempting believers to get back under the Law of Moses. His answer is the same for both—we are sons now, being transformed from the inside out by the Spirit, so why would you want to return to the infant ways of the Law? The Law was a tutor to bring us to sonship, not the other way around.

[13]Marvin R. Vincent, *Word Studies in the New Testament* (Peabody, MA: Hendrickson, 1985).

[14]Howard Gardner, *Frames of Mind: Theory of Multiple Intelligence* (New York: Basic Books, 1993).

[15]Michael Ray, as interviewed in Peter Senge, *Presence: Human Purpose and the Field of the Future* (New York: Crown Publishing/Random House, 2004), 30.

[16]The CDC-Kaiser Permanente Adverse Childhood Experiences (ACE) Study is one of the largest investigations of childhood abuse and neglect and later-life health and well-being. The original ACE Study was conducted at Kaiser Permanente from 1995 to 1997 with two waves of data collection. Over 17,000 Health Maintenance Organization members from Southern California receiving physical exams completed confidential surveys regarding their childhood experiences and current health status and behaviors.

More detailed information about the study can be found in Vincent J Felitti et al., "Relationship of Childhood Abuse and Household Dysfunction to Many of the Leading Causes of Death in Adults," *American Journal of Preventive Medicine* 14, no. 4 (May 1998): 245–258, or via the links provided in Centers for Disease Control and Prevention, "About the CDC-Kaiser ACE Study," CDC, last modified June 14, 2016, accessed November 11, 2017, https://www.cdc.gov/violenceprevention/acestudy/about.html.

[17]Dose-response is a measurement of the relationship between the quantity of a substance or exposure [e.g. radiation], (the dose) and its overall effect (the response). Graphing the pattern of physiological response to varied dosage.

[18]Nadine Burke Harris, "How Childhood Trauma Affects Health Across a Lifetime," *TEDMED* 2014, published September 2014, accessed November 15, 2017, https://www.ted.com/talks/nadine_burke_harris_how_childhood_trauma_affects_health_across_a_lifetime.

[19]Ibid.

[20]Don't miss the fact that God's redemptive story with man begins in a lush garden lacking nothing, and ends in one as well (Gen. 2:8-10 and Rev. 22:1-2). The critical decision is in the Garden of Gethsemane and the triumph is on display in the garden of Joseph of Arimathea's tomb. In the Scriptures, gardens have always represented the highest will and purpose of God for man. Think about that.

[21]William Paul Young and Brian Robison, *The Shack: Where Tragedy Confronts Eternity* (Newbury Park, CA: Windblown Media, 2007). His follow-up fiction called "Cross Roads" uses the same imagery of the inner soul of a man being explored by the man himself with a guide that interprets for him what he is seeing about himself. "Lies That We Believe About God" is the plain language of both novels.

[22]Richard C. Francis, *Epigenetics: How Environment Shapes Our Genes* (New York: W.W. Norton and Co., 2011), xi.

[23]Janet G. Woititz, *The Adult Children of Alcoholics* (Deerfield Beach, FL: Health Communications, Inc., 1983), and The Intimacy Struggle (Deerfield Beach, FL: Health Communications, Inc. 1993).

[24]Francis, Richard C. *Epigenetics: How Environment Shapes Our Genes.* New York: W.W. Norton and Co., 2011. p. 159.

[25]William P. Young, *The Shack*, 137.

[26]Fee, Paul, *The Spirit and the People of God*, 69.

[27]A great Bible study project for you or your Home Fellowship Group is to survey the fifty-eight "one another's" in Paul's writings. These alone will broaden our perspective to see that our Triune relational God is not cultivating a few super-stars, but a body of inter-dependent saints who are linked together in heart and purpose by the Holy Spirit.

[28]Tracy Goss, *The Last Word on Power* (New York: Doubleday, 1996), 19.

[29]Martin Heidegger, *Being and Time* (New York: Harper Collins, 2008), 203-210. Heidegger has understood language as "the house of being." The implications of Heidegger's proposal thoughts have suggested that "being" could be altered through the conversations (listening and speaking) in which one has engaged.

Goss (*The Last Word on Power* (New York: Doubleday, 1996)) says, "The idea of changing your actions (and the events in the world around you) through conversation feels alien for many people, partly because it is so abstract, and partly because it contradicts … a person's personality. From a psychological perspective, actions stem from deeply seated motives … Psychologically, no one can really alter those deep motives except, perhaps, through years of arduous analysis. From an ontological perspective, by contrast, everything is apparent in the conversation being held at that moment. This gives everyone a starting place for making dramatic alterations and the tools for doing so. By learning to uncover the concealed aspects of your current conversations and learning to engage in different types of new conversation, you can alter the way you are being, which, in turn, alters what's possible. When you create a new context, you create a new realm of possibility, one that did not previously exist."

Could it be that God has so designed mankind and creation in the reality of sound (i.e., upholding all things by His word) that language has, in fact, served as a type of "creative speech" with real implications for increasing trust and changes a person's reality?

[30]U.S. Diplomacy Center, "Why Do Diplomats Give Gifts?" *Discover Diplomacy*, accessed April 3, 2018, https://diplomacy.state.gov/discoverdiplomacy/diplomacy101/people/203502.htm.

[31]Robert Morris, *The God I Never Knew* (Colorado Springs: Water Brook Press, 2011).

[32]Jack W. Hayford, *The Beauty of Spiritual Language* (Nashville: Thomas Nelson, 1996).

[33]Fee, *GOD's Empowering Presence*.

[34]Caroline Leaf, "Prayer Blocks Toxic Thoughts" YouTube (Grace Gleanings Ministries) published June 23, 2016, accessed December 2017, https://www.youtube.com/watch?v=rB07pecRv7U

[35]Andrew Newberg and Mark Robert Waldman. *How God Changes Your Brain: Breakthrough Findings from a Leading Neuroscientist* (New York: Ballentine Books, 2010).

[36]Jack W. Hayford, ed. *The Hayford Bible Handbook* (Nashville: Thomas Nelson, 1995), 793.

[37]Benedict Carey, "Speech Guided by Faith, Not Will: Study Indicates Language, Thinking Centers of Brain Are Quiet during State of 'Speaking in Tongues,'" *Houston Chronicle*, November 11, 2006, Religion, 1, accessed May 13, 2009. http://www.chron.com/CDA/archives/archive.mpl?id=2006_4227258.

[38]A good example of Luke's writing style is seen in Paul's conversion story of Acts 9. Because Luke has set the lens upon the entire book as the promise (chapter 1) and fulfillment (chapter 2) of the outpouring of the Spirit, he presumes the reader understands this is now the norm in the church. It is normal to be saved, baptized in water and filled with the Spirit (Acts 2:39). He documents that Ananias has been sent to Saul in Damascus to lay hands on him that his eyes would be opened and that he would be baptized with the Holy Spirit since his conversion (Acts 9). He records that scales fall from Paul's eyes but says nothing about him receiving Spirit Baptism. Why not? Because it is assumed as the norm in the early Church. Paul later affirms that he was baptized in the Spirit by telling the Corinthians, "I thank my God I speak in tongues more than all of you" (1 Cor. 14:18). When he discovers believers from Ephesus who are not baptized in the Spirit, he readily corrects the abnormality (Acts 19:1-7). Luke doesn't feel the necessity to document that every time people were baptized in the Spirit they spoke in tongues; it was assumed – it was normal.

[39]D. A. Tappeiner, "The Function of Tongue-Speaking for the Individual: A Psycho-Theological Model," *Journal of the American Scientific Affiliation* 26, (1974): 32. Quoting from the MMPI: Minnesota Multi-Phasic Personality Indicator.

[40]For further along this line study read "Prayer that Enlarges Millions" in Jack W. Hayford, *Prayer is Invading the Impossible* (Alachua, FL: Bridge-Logos Publishers, 1977), 159-172.

[41]MMPI: Minnesota Multi-Phasic Personality Indicator, 1973.

[42]Ibid.

[43]Tappeiner, "The Function of Tongue-Speaking for the Individual," 32.

[44]Raymond T. Brock, "The Therapeutic Value of Speaking in Tongues," *Paraclete Journal* 23, no. 1 (1989): 24.

[45]Tappeiner, "The Function of Tongue-Speaking for the Individual," 32.

[46]Morton T. Kelsey, *Tongue Speaking: An Experiment in Spiritual Experience* (Garden City, NY: Doubleday, 1968).

[47]Hayford, *The Beauty of Spiritual Language*. Some refer to the categories of the nine manifestation gifts (1 Cor. 12) as revelation, utterance, and power. Some use discerning, declaring, and dynamic. Hayford's are as clear as any, *revelation, communication* and *power*.

[48]Jesus said, "No one comes to the Father except by me" (John 14:6). This includes even the Jews who died in faith under the Older Covenant. This is underscored by the fact that Old Testament saints, upon death, went to "Abraham's Bosom" or "Paradise" where they waited in comfort for Messiah to come and redeem mankind by His blood. Upon Jesus' resurrection many of the graves of the Old Testament saints open, and those who had been waiting in Paradise took one final tour of the Old City before going to the New one (Matt. 27:52). No one goes to the Father except through Jesus.

[49]When my children were younger it always took longer to get somewhere with 5 or 6 in the car then it did with just one or two! I could typically add thirty minutes per child to the total travel time for longer one-day road trips.

[50]Since praying in the S/spirit (aka "praying/speaking in tongues"), is not speaking to men, it does not require interpretation. It differs from the message in tongues given in a public meeting ("the gift of tongues") which should be interpreted "so that all may praise God and be strengthened" (1 Cor. 14:5). I am indebted to Phil Strickland, learned friend, for this clarification.

[51]Fee, *GOD's Empowering Presence*, 148.

[52]Substance Abuse and Mental Health Services Administration, "Results from the 2012 National Survey on Drug Use and Health: Summary of National Findings," *NSDUH Series H-46*, (SMA) 13-4795 (Rockville, MD: Substance Abuse and Mental Health Services Administration, 2013). https://www.samhsa.gov/data/sites/default/files/NSDUHresults2012/NSDUHresults2012.pdf

[53]David J. Bosch, *Transforming Mission: Paradigm Shifts in Theology of Mission* (Maryknoll, NY: Orbis Books, 2011) 389-390.

[54]David Seamands, *Ministry in the Image of God: The Trinitarian Shape of Christian Service* (Downers Grove: InterVarsity Press, 2005)157-178.

[55]Jürgen Moltmann, *The Church in the Power of the Spirit: A Contribution to Messianic Ecclesiology*, trans. Margaret Kohl (Minneapolis: Fortress Press, 1993).

[56]It is entirely possible that my childhood pastors and teachers were saying all of these things. Either I just wasn't listening, or I didn't have ears to hear it.

[57]Michael J. McClymond, *Encounters with God: An Approach to the Theology of Jonathan Edwards* (Oxford: Oxford University Press, 1998), 56.

[58]Mark Hanby. *You Have Not Many Fathers.* Destiny Publishing, 1995.5

[59]Ray S. Anderson, *The Soul of Ministry* (Louisville: Westminster John Knox Press, 1997), 154-155.

[60]See Don Richardson, *Eternity in Their Hearts*, a documentation of the Spirit preceding the Church into many cultures to prepare them for the coming Good News. (Bloomington, MN: Bethany House Publishers, 1981).

[61]Henri J. M. Nouwen. *Spiritual Formation: Following the Movements of the Spirit* (New York: Harper Collins, 2010), 34.

[62]These points were inspired by a social media post from Ben Hughes, Australia, 2017, edited and adapted.

[63]Jesus connects "keeping the commandments" with the Father and Son coming to them … this is addressed in the final chapter: "Redefining the Terms."

[64]Wayne Cordeiro, *The Divine Mentor: Growing Your Faith as You Sit at the Feet of the Savior* (Bloomington, MN: Bethany House, 2007).

"Todd White," *Lifestyle Christianity*, last modified 2018, accessed February 2018, https://lifestylechristianity.com/about/.

[65]Warren Farrell and John Gray, *The Boy Crisis: Why Our Boys are Struggling and What We Can Do About It* (Dallas: BenBella Books, Inc., 2018).

[66]Saul Alinsky, *Rules for Radicals: A Primer for Realistic Radicals* (New York: Random House, 1971), xviii.

[67]Mark's Gospel is known as "the memoirs of Peter." What we read in Mark are Peter's recollection of the works and sayings of Jesus as Peter told them to Mark. A number of commentaries on the Gospel of Mark will give added explanation. See especially "Gospel of Mark" in David Pawson, *Unlocking the Bible* (Travelers Rest, SC: True Potential Publishing, Inc., 2017), 483-492.

[68]Mark 7:24-30. It is no accident that Mark immediately follows Jesus statement about foods being cleansed with two accounts of Jesus healing Gentiles. Jesus goes to Tyre and Sidon and delivers the daughter of a Greek Syro-Phoenecian woman. Then He went to the Decapolis (a 10-cities area where the Roman military retired) and delivered the man with a deaf and dumb spirit (Mark 10:31-37). Peter is showing us through Mark's Gospel that Jesus' ministry was demonstrating God's

love to all ethnicities and nationalities equally, that no man was to be called unclean?

[70]Consider that years after the Acts 10 experience at Cornelius' house, and Peter's subsequent testimony to the leaders of the Church in Jerusalem (Acts 15:7, 8), that Peter still had tendencies to fall back into old religious mindsets of respecting the Jewish laws of separation over the revelation of Jesus, and Paul rebukes Peter publicly "to his face" (Gal. 2:11, 12).

[71]To "Keep" (Greek: *tereō*): Attention, to ward off, to watch over, to guard carefully, to observe. Kittel and Friedrich, *Theological Dictionary of the New Testament*, 1174-75.

Bibliography

Alinsky, Saul. *Rules for Radicals: A Primer for Realistic Radicals.* New York: Random House, 1971.

Anderson, Ray S. *The Soul of Ministry.* Louisville: Westminster John Knox Press, 1997.

Bosch, David J. *Transforming Mission: Paradigm Shifts in Theology of Mission.* Maryknoll, NY: Orbis Books, 2011.

Brock, Raymond T. "The Therapeutic Value of Speaking in Tongues." Paraclete Journal 23, No. 1 (1989).

Burke Harris, Nadine. "How Childhood Trauma Affects Health Across a Lifetime." TEDMED 2014. Published September 2014. Accessed November 15, 2017. https://www.ted.com/talks/nadine_burke_harris_how_childhood_trauma_affects_health_across_a_lifetime.

Carey, Benedict. "Speech Guided by Faith, Not Will / Study Indicates Language, Thinking Centers of Brain Are Quiet during State of 'Speaking in Tongues.'" Houston Chronicle, November 11, 2006, Religion, 1. Accessed May 13, 2009. http://www.chron.com/CDA/archives/archive.mpl?id=2006_4227258.

Chan. Francis. *Forgotten God: Reversing Our Tragic Neglect of the Holy Spirit.* Colorado Springs, David C. Cook, 2009.

———. *Remembering the Forgotten God.* Colorado Springs: David C. Cook Publishing, 2010

Cordeiro, Wayne. *The Divine Mentor: Growing Your Faith as You Sit at the Feet of the Savior.* Bloomington, MN: Bethany House, 2007.

Farrell, Warren and John Gray. *The Boy Crisis: Why Our Boys are Struggling and What We Can Do About It.* Dallas: BenBella Books, Inc., 2018.

Fee, Gordon D. *GOD's Empowering Presence: The Holy Spirit in the Letters of Paul.* Peabody, MA: Hendrickson, 1994.

———. *Paul, The Spirit and the People of God.* Grand Rapids: Baker Academic, 1996.

Felitti, Vincent J. et al., "Relationship of Childhood Abuse and Household Dysfunction to Many of the Leading Causes of Death in Adults." *American Journal of Preventive Medicine* 14, no. 4 (May 1998): 245–258.

Francis, Richard C. *Epigenetics: How Environment Shapes Our Genes.* New York: W. W. Norton and Co., 2011.

Gardner, Howard. *Frames of Mind: Theory of Multiple Intelligence.* New York: Basic Books, 1993.

Goss, Tracy. *The Last Word on Power*. New York: Doubleday, 1996.

Hanby. Mark. *You Have Not Many Fathers*. Destiny Publishing, 1995.

Hayford, Jack W. *Prayer is Invading the Impossible*. Alachua, FL: Bridge-Logos Publishers, 1977.

———. *The Beauty of Spiritual Language*. Nashville: Thomas Nelson, 1996.

Hayford, Jack W., ed. *The Hayford Bible Handbook*. Nashville, Thomas Nelson, 1995.

Heidegger, Martin. *Being and Time*. New York: Harper Collins, 2008.

Kelsey, Morton T. *Tongue Speaking: An Experiment in Spiritual Experience*. Garden City, NY: Doubleday, 1968.

Kittel, Gerhard and Gerhard Friedrich, eds. *Theological Dictionary of the New Testament*. Grand Rapids: Eerdmans, 1985.

Leaf, Caroline. "Prayer Blocks Toxic Thoughts." YouTube (Grace Gleanings Ministries). Published June 23, 2016. Accessed December 2017, https://www.youtube.com/watch?v=rB07pecRv7U

McClymond, Michael J. *Encounters with God: An Approach to the Theology of Jonathan Edwards*. Oxford: Oxford University Press, 1998.

Moltmann, Jürgen. *The Church in the Power of the Spirit: A Contribution to Messianic Ecclesiology*. Translated by Margaret Kohl. Minneapolis: Fortress Press, 1993.

Morris, Robert. *The God I Never Knew*. Colorado Springs: Water Brook Press, 2011.

Newberg, Andrew and Mark Robert Waldman. *How God Changes Your Brain: Breakthrough Findings from a Leading Neuroscientist*. New York: Ballentine Books, 2020.

Nouwen, Henri J. M. *Spiritual Formation: Following the Movements of the Spirit*. New York: Harper Collins, 2010.

Pawson, David. *Unlocking the Bible*. Travelers Rest, SC: True Potential Publishing, Inc., 2017.

Richardson, Don. *Eternity in Their Hearts*. Bloomington, MN: Bethany House Publishers, 1981.

Seamands, David. *Ministry in the Image of God: The Trinitarian Shape of Christian Service*. Downers Grove: InterVarsity Press, 2005.

Senge, Peter. *Presence: Human Purpose and the Field of the Future*. New York: Crown Publishing / Random House, 2004.

Substance Abuse and Mental Health Services Administration. "Results from the 2012 National Survey on Drug Use and Health: Summary of National Findings." *NSDUH Series* H-46. (SMA) 13-4795. Rockville, MD: Substance Abuse and Mental Health Services Administration, 2013.

Tappeiner, D. A. "The Function of Tongue-Speaking for the Individual: A Psycho-Theological Model." *Journal of the American Scientific Affiliation* 26. (1974): 32.

"Todd White." *Lifestyle Christianity.* Last modified 2018. Accessed February 2018. https://lifestylechristianity.com/about/.

U.S. Diplomacy Center. "Why Do Diplomats Give Gifts?" *Discover Diplomacy.* Accessed April 3, 2018. https://diplomacy.state.gov/discoverdiplomacy/diplomacy101/people/203502.htm

Unger, Merrill F. *Unger's Bible Dictionary.* Chicago: Moody Press, 1979.

Vincent, Marvin R. *Word Studies in the New Testament.* Peabody, MA: Hendrickson, 1985.

Woititz, Janet G. *The Adult Children of Alcoholics.* Deerfield Beach, FL: Health Communications, Inc., 1983.

———. *The Intimacy Struggle.* Deerfield Beach, FL: Health Communications, Inc. 1993.

Wood, Chiqui. *The Abba Foundation.* Bedford, TX: Burkhart Books, 2018.

Wood, Kerry. *The Abba Factor.* Bedford, TX: Burkhart Books, 2018.

———. *The Gifts of the Spirit for a New Generation.* Zadok Publishing, 2015.

William Paul Young and Brian Robison. *The Shack: Where Tragedy Confronts Eternity.* Newbury Park, CA: Windblown Media, 2007.

About the Author

Kerry Wood is passionate about authentic Christianity lived in the power of the Spirit. In over thirty-five years of pastoral ministry he has focused on the local church, prayer movements, and community transformation initiatives. He has launched or sponsored several church plants in the U.S. and abroad and has spoken in leadership conferences, crusades, and local churches in more than twenty countries and throughout the U.S. He has authored a variety of ministry materials, published articles, Bible curricula- and audio-video teaching.

As a local church leader, seminary professor and member of the Society of Pentecostal Studies, Kerry is committed to partnership with Holy Spirit, intercessory prayer, teaching the Word, five-fold equipping of the Church, leadership development and church planting. He endeavors to steward partnership with the Holy Spirit through the gifts, and introducing people to Spirit Baptism. His philosophy of life and ministry is about "being" before 'doing', an overflow of God's fullness as the source of all activity.

Kerry holds a Doctor of Ministry and Master of Divinity from The King's University (Los Angeles), a Masters of Arts in Biblical Literature from the Assemblies of God Theological Seminary, and Bachelors in Christian Ministry from Southwestern Assemblies of God University.

Kerry is married to (Dr.) Ana (Chiqui) Wood, and has four grown children, Robert, Geoffrey, Audrea, and Lauren.

www.DrKerryWood.com

www.TableofFriends.com

Check out the other two books in the trilogy:

THE ABBA FOUNDATION:
True freedom from the orphan spirit is impossible without a right view of God.

THE ABBA FACTOR:
Sonship is not a place to get to—but a way to be; seeing yourself through the Father's eyes radically sets one free from the orphan lies.